SCIENTIFIC AMERICAN EXPLORES BIG IDEAS

The Origins of Humanity

The Editors of *Scientific American*

SCIENTIFIC AMERICAN EDUCATIONAL PUBLISHING
New York

Published in 2024 by Scientific American Educational Publishing
in association with **The Rosen Publishing Group**
2544 Clinton Street, Buffalo NY 14224

Contains material from Scientific American®, a division of Springer Nature America, Inc., reprinted by permission, as well as original material from The Rosen Publishing Group®.

First Edition

Scientific American
Lisa Pallatroni: Project Editor

Rosen Publishing
Daniel R. Faust: Compiling Editor
Michael Moy: Senior Graphic Designer

Cataloging-in-Publication Data

Names: Scientific American, Inc.
Title: The origins of humanity / edited by the Scientific American Editors.
Description: First Edition. | New York : Scientific American Educational Publishing, 2024. | Series: Scientific American explores big ideas | Includes glossary and index.
Identifiers: ISBN 9781725349636 (pbk.) | ISBN 9781725349643 (library bound)| ISBN 9781725349650 (ebook)
Subjects: LCSH: Human beings–Juvenile literature. | Life (Biology)–Juvenile literature. | Life–Origin–Juvenile literature. | Evolution–Juvenile literature.Genetics–Juvenile literature.
Classification: LCC GN31.5 O754 2024 | DDC 576–dc23

Manufactured in the United States of America
Websites listed were live at the time of publication.

Cover: JuliusKielaitis/Shutterstock.com

CPSIA Compliance Information: Batch # SACS24.

For Further Information contact Rosen Publishing at 1-800-237-9932.

CONTENTS

INTRODUCTION

Where do we come from? Why are humans different from all the other animals that share our planet? What makes us . . . us? Is it the size of our brains or the fact that we walk upright? Scientists have been trying to answer these questions for over a hundred years. The articles that follow explore the origins of *Homo sapiens*, from the biological evolution of the modern human to the cultural development of language, the arts, and technology. Readers will be introduced to humanity's earliest ancestors, like *Australopithecus* and *Homo habilis*, and discover what separates them from modern humans. How accurate is the familiar image of the brutish caveman, and are we really that different from our Neandertal cousins? The answers to some of these questions might be obvious, but others may surprise you.

In Section 1, "Being Human," the articles examine the anatomical evolution of humans and the differences between modern humans and our hominid ancestors. Section 2, "What Makes Us Human?," explores how these evolutionary changes make modern humans unique, as well as the ways these changes helped humans spread across the globe and become the dominant species on the planet. How did the development of language and technology alter the trajectory of humanity? What role did art play in humanity's earliest days? Section 3, "Invention and Innovation," takes a deep dive into the history of human culture to answer these questions and discover whether they are truly unique to humans. Section 4, "You Are What You Eat," looks at how our early ancestors' diet may have played a role in the development of modern humans.

Section 1: Being Human

Why Is *Homo sapiens* the Sole Surviving Member of the Human Family?

By Kate Wong

At the dawning of *Homo sapiens*, our ancestors were born into a world we would find utterly surreal. It's not so much that the climate and sea levels or the plants and the animals were different, although of course they were–it's that there were other kinds of humans alive at the same time. For most of *H. sapiens*' existence, in fact, multiple human species walked the earth. In Africa, where our species got its start, large-brained *Homo heidelbergensis* and small-brained *Homo naledi* also roamed. In Asia, there was *Homo erectus*, a mysterious group dubbed the Denisovans and, later, *Homo floresiensis*–a hobbitlike creature, tiny but for its large feet. The stocky, heavy-browed Neandertals, for their part, ruled Europe and western Asia. And there were probably even more forms, as yet undiscovered.

By around 40,000 years ago, based on current evidence, *H. sapiens* found itself all alone, the only remaining member of what was once an incredibly diverse family of bipedal primates, together known as hominins. (In this article, the terms "human" and "hominin" both refer to *H. sapiens* and its extinct relatives.) How did our kind come to be the last human standing?

Until a few years ago, scientists favored a simple explanation: *H. sapiens* arose relatively recently, in more or less its current form, in a single region of Africa and spread out from there into the rest of the Old World, supplanting the Neandertals and other archaic human species it encountered along the way. There was no appreciable interspecies fraternizing, just wholesale replacement of the old guards by the clever newcomer, whose ascendancy seemed inevitable.

Yet mounting evidence from fossil and archaeological discoveries, as well as DNA analyses, has experts increasingly rethinking that scenario. It now looks as though *H. sapiens* originated far earlier than previously thought, possibly in locations across Africa instead of a single region, and that some of its distinguishing traits—including aspects of the brain—evolved piecemeal. Moreover, it has become abundantly clear that *H. sapiens* actually did mingle with the other human species it encountered and that interbreeding with them may have been a crucial factor in our success. Together these findings paint a far more complex picture of our origins than many researchers had envisioned—one that privileges the role of dumb luck over destiny in the success of our kind.

Theory Under Threat

Debate about the origin of our species has traditionally focused on two competing models. On one side was the Recent African Origin hypothesis, championed by paleoanthropologist Christopher Stringer and others, which argues that *H. sapiens* arose in either eastern or southern Africa within the past 200,000 years and, because of its inherent superiority, subsequently replaced archaic hominin species around the globe without interbreeding with them to any significant degree. On the other was the Multiregional Evolution model, formulated by paleoanthropologists Milford Wolpoff, Xinzhi Wu and Alan Thorne, which holds that modern *H. sapiens* evolved from Neandertals and other archaic human populations throughout the Old World, which were connected through migration and mating. In this view, *H. sapiens* has far deeper roots, reaching back nearly 2 million years.

By the early 2000s, the Recent African Origin model had a wealth of evidence in its favor. Analyses of the DNA of living people indicated that our species originated no more than 200,000 years ago. The earliest known fossils attributed to our species came from two sites in Ethiopia, Omo and Herto, dated to around 195,000 and 160,000 years ago, respectively. And sequences of mitochondrial DNA (the tiny loop of genetic material found in the cell's power plants, which is different from the DNA contained in the cell's nucleus) recovered from Neandertal fossils were distinct from the mitochondrial DNA of people today–exactly as one would expect if *H. sapiens* replaced archaic human species without mating with them.

Not all of the evidence fit with this tidy story, however. Many archaeologists think that the start of a cultural phase known as the Middle Stone Age (MSA) heralded the emergence of people who were beginning to think like us. Prior to this technological shift, archaic human species throughout the Old World made pretty much the same kinds of stone tools fashioned in the so-called Acheulean style. Acheulean technology centered on the production of hefty hand axes that were made by taking a chunk of stone and chipping away at it until it had the desired shape.

With the onset of the MSA, our ancestors adopted a new approach to toolmaking, inverting the knapping process to focus on the small, sharp flakes they detached from the core–a more efficient use of raw material that required sophisticated planning. And they began attaching these sharp flakes to handles to create spears and other projectile weapons. Moreover, some people who made MSA tools also made items associated with symbolic behavior, including shell beads for jewelry and pigment for painting. A reliance on symbolic behavior, including language, is thought to be one of the hallmarks of the modern mind.

The problem was that the earliest dates for the MSA were more than 250,000 years ago–far older than those for the earliest *H. sapiens* fossils at less than 200,000 years ago. Did another human species invent the MSA, or did *H. sapiens* actually evolve far earlier than the fossils seemed to indicate?

In 2010, another wrinkle emerged. Geneticists announced that they had recovered nuclear DNA from Neandertal fossils and sequenced it. Nuclear DNA makes up the bulk of our genetic material. Comparison of the Neandertal nuclear DNA with that of living people revealed that non-African people today carry DNA from Neandertals, showing that *H. sapiens* and Neandertals did interbreed after all, at least on occasion.

Subsequent ancient genome studies confirmed that Neandertals contributed to the modern human gene pool, as did other archaic humans. Further, contrary to the notion that *H. sapiens* originated within the past 200,000 years, the ancient DNA suggested that Neandertals and *H. sapiens* diverged from their common ancestor considerably earlier than that, perhaps upward of half a million years ago. If so, *H. sapiens* might have originated more than twice as long ago as the fossil record indicated.

Ancient Roots

Recent discoveries at a site called Jebel Irhoud in Morocco have helped bring the fossil, cultural and genetic evidence into better alignment–and bolstered a new view of our origins. When barite miners first discovered fossils at the site back in 1961, anthropologists thought the bones were around 40,000 years old and belonged to Neandertals. But over the years, continued excavations and analyses led researchers to revise that assessment. In June 2017, paleoanthropologist Jean-Jacques Hublin of the Max Planck Institute for Evolutionary Anthropology in Leipzig, Germany, and his colleagues announced that they had recovered additional fossils from the site, along with MSA tools. Using two dating techniques, they estimated the remains to be roughly 315,000 years old. The researchers had found the oldest traces of *H. sapiens* to date, as well as the oldest traces of MSA culture–pushing back the fossil evidence of our species by more than 100,000 years and linking it to the earliest known appearance of the MSA.

Not everyone agrees that the Jebel Irhoud fossils belong to *H. sapiens*. Some experts think they may instead come from a close relative. But if Hublin and his collaborators are right about the identity of the bones, the constellation of skull traits that distinguish *H. sapiens* from other human species did not all emerge in lockstep at the inception of our kind, as supporters of the Recent African Origin theory had supposed. The fossils resemble modern humans in having a small face, for example. But the braincase is elongated like those of archaic human species rather than rounded like our own dome. This shape difference reflects differences in brain organization: compared with fully modern humans, the Jebel Irhoud individuals had smaller parietal lobes, which process sensory input, and a smaller cerebellum, which is involved in language and social cognition, among other functions.

Neither do the archaeological remains at Jebel Irhoud exhibit the full complement of MSA features. The people there made MSA stone tools for hunting and butchering gazelles that roamed the grasslands that once carpeted this now desert landscape. And they built fires, probably to cook their food and warm themselves against the chill of night. But they did not leave behind any traces of symbolic expression.

In fact, on the whole, they are not especially more sophisticated than the Neandertals or *H. heidelbergensis*. If you could journey back in time to our species' debut, you wouldn't necessarily pick it to win the evolutionary sweepstakes. Although early *H. sapiens* had some innovations, "there weren't any big changes at 300,000 years ago that indicate they were destined to be successful," observes archaeologist Michael Petraglia of the Max Planck Institute for the Science of Human History in Jena, Germany. "In the beginning with *sapiens*," Petraglia says, "it looks like anyone's game."

Gardens of Eden

The total *H. sapiens* package, many researchers agree, did not coalesce until sometime between 100,000 and 40,000 years ago. So what happened in the intervening 200,000 years or more to transform our species from run-of-the-mill hominin to world-conquering force of nature? Scientists are increasingly thinking about how the size and structure of the early *H. sapiens* population might have factored into the metamorphosis. In a paper published online in 2018 in *Trends in Ecology & Evolution*, archaeologist Eleanor Scerri of the University of Oxford and a large interdisciplinary group of co-authors, including Stringer, make the case for what they call the African Multiregionalism model of *H. sapiens* evolution. The scientists note that the earliest putative members of our species—namely, the Jebel Irhoud fossils from Morocco, the Herto and Omo

Kibish fossils from Ethiopia, and a partial skull from Florisbad, South Africa–all look far more different from one another than people today do. So much so that some researchers have argued that they belong to different species or subspecies. "But maybe early *H. sapiens* was just ridiculously diverse," Scerri offers. And maybe looking for a single point of origin for our species, as many researchers have been doing, is "a wild goose chase," she says.

When Scerri and her colleagues examined the latest data from fossils, DNA and archaeology, the emergence of *H. sapiens* began to look less like a single origin story and more like a pan-African phenomenon. Rather than evolving as a small population in a particular region of Africa, they propose, our species emerged from a large population that was subdivided into smaller groups distributed across the vast African continent that were often semi-isolated for thousands of years at a time by distance and by ecological barriers such as deserts. Those bouts of solitude allowed each group to develop its own biological and technological adaptations to its own niche, be it an arid woodland or a savanna grassland, a tropical rain forest or a marine coast. Every so often, however, the groups came into contact with one another, allowing for both genetic and cultural exchange that fed the evolution of our lineage.

Shifting climate could have fueled the fracturing and rejoining of the subpopulations. For instance, paleoenvironmental data have shown that every 100,000 years or so, Africa enters into a humid phase that transforms the forbidding Sahara Desert into a lush expanse of vegetation and lakes. These green Sahara episodes, as they are known, would have allowed populations formerly isolated by the harsh desert to link up. When the Sahara dried out again, populations would be sequestered anew and able to undergo their own evolutionary experiments for another stretch of time until the next greening.

A population subdivided into groups that each adapted to their own ecological niche, even as occasional migration between groups kept them connected, would explain not only the mosaic evolution of *H. sapiens'* distinctive anatomy but also the patchwork pattern of the MSA, Scerri and her co-authors argue. Unlike Acheulean tools, which look mostly the same everywhere they turn up throughout the Old World, MSA tools exhibit considerable regional variation. Sites spanning the time between 130,000 and 60,000 years ago in North Africa, for example, contain tool types not found at sites in South Africa from the same interval, including stone implements bearing distinctive stems that may have served as attachment points for handles. Likewise, South African sites contain slender, leaf-shaped tools made of stone that was heated to improve its fracture mechanics–no such implements appear in the North African record. Complex technology and symbolism become more common over time across the continent, but each group acts its own way, tailoring its culture to its specific niche and customs.

H. sapiens was not the only hominin evolving bigger brains and sophisticated behaviors, however. Hublin notes that human fossils from China dating to between 300,000 and 50,000 years ago, which he suspects belong to Denisovans, exhibit increased brain size. And Neandertals invented complex tools, as well as their own forms of symbolic expression and social connectedness, over the course of their long reign. But such behaviors do not appear to have become as highly developed or as integral to their way of life as they eventually did in ours, observes archaeologist John Shea of Stony Brook University, who thinks that advanced language skills allowed *H. sapiens* to prevail.

"All these groups are evolving in the same direction," Hublin says. "But our species crosses a threshold before the others in terms of cognitive ability, social complexity and reproductive success." And when it does–around 50,000 years ago, in Hublin's estimation–"the boiling milk escapes the saucepan." Forged and honed in Africa, *H. sapiens* could now enter virtually any environment on the earth and thrive. It was unstoppable.

Close Encounters

Hundreds of thousands of years of splitting up from and reuniting with members of our own species might have given *H. sapiens* an edge over other members of the human family. But it was not the only factor in our rise to world domination. We may actually owe our extinct relatives a substantial debt of gratitude for their contributions to our success. The archaic human species that *H. sapiens* met as it migrated within Africa and beyond its borders were not merely competitors–they were also mates. The proof lies in the DNA of people today: Neandertal DNA makes up some 2 percent of the genomes of Eurasians; Denisovan DNA composes up to 5 percent of the DNA of Melanesians. And a recent study by Arun Durvasula and Sriram Sankararaman, both at the University of California, Los Angeles, found that nearly 8 percent of the genetic ancestry of the West African Yoruba population traces back to an unknown archaic species. Other genetic evidence from contemporary populations suggests that *H. sapiens* also interbred with unknown extinct hominins in South and East Asia.

Some of the DNA that *H. sapiens* picked up from archaic hominins may have helped our species adapt to the novel habitats it entered on its march across the globe. When geneticist Joshua Akey of Princeton University and his colleagues studied the Neandertal sequences in modern human populations, they found 15 that occur at high frequencies, a sign that they had beneficial consequences. These high-frequency sequences cluster into two groups. About half of them influence immunity. "As modern humans dispersed into new environments, they were exposed to new pathogens and viruses," Akey says. Through interbreeding, "they could have picked up adaptations from Neandertals that were better able to fight off those new pathogens," he explains.

The other half of the Neandertal sequences that Akey's team found at high frequency in modern human populations are related to skin, including genes that influence pigmentation levels. Researchers have previously theorized that *H. sapiens* individuals from Africa, who presumably had darker skin to protect against harmful ultraviolet radiation from the sun, would have had to evolve lighter skin as they entered northern latitudes to get enough vitamin D, which the body acquires mainly through sun exposure.

Skin genes from Neandertals may have aided our predecessors in doing exactly that.

Neandertals are not the only archaic humans who gave us useful genes. For example, modern-day Tibetans have the Denisovans to thank for a gene variant that helps them cope with the low-oxygen environment of the high-altitude Tibetan plateau. And contemporary African populations have inherited from an unknown archaic ancestor a variant of a gene that may help fend off bad bacteria inside the mouth.

Interbreeding with archaic humans who had millennia to evolve adaptations to local conditions may well have allowed invading *H. sapiens* to adjust to novel environments faster than if it had to wait for favorable mutations to crop up in its own gene pool. But it's not all upside. Some of the genes we obtained from Neandertals are associated with depression and other diseases. Perhaps these genes were advantageous in the past and only began causing trouble in the context of modern ways of life. Or maybe, Akey suggests, the risk of developing these diseases was a tolerable price to pay for the benefits these genes conferred.

Archaic humans may have contributed more than DNA to our species. Researchers have argued that contact between divergent human groups probably led to cultural exchange and may have even spurred innovation. For example, the arrival of *H. sapiens* in western Europe, where the Neandertals long resided, coincided with an uncharacteristic burst of technological and artistic creativity in both groups. Previously some experts suggested that Neandertals were simply aping the inventive newcomers. But maybe it was the interaction between the two groups that ignited the cultural explosion on both sides.

In a sense, the fact that *H. sapiens* mixed with other human lineages should not come as a surprise. "We know from many animals that hybridization has played an important role in evolution," observes biological anthropologist Rebecca Rogers Ackermann of the University of Cape Town in South Africa. "In some cases, it can create populations, and even new species, that are better adapted to new or changing environments than their parents were because of novel traits or novel combinations of traits." Human ancestors show a similar pattern: the combination of different lineages resulted in the adaptable, variable species we are today. "*Homo sapiens* is the product of a complex interplay of lineages," Ackermann asserts, and it has flourished precisely because of the variation that arose from this interplay. "Without it," she says, "we simply wouldn't be as successful."

How often such mingling occurred and the extent to which it helped drive evolution in *H. sapiens* and other hominins remain to be determined. But it may be that the particular environmental and demographic circumstances in which our species found itself in Africa and abroad led to more opportunities for genetic and cultural exchange with other groups than our fellow hominins experienced. We got lucky—and are no less marvelous for it.

Referenced

The Hybrid Origin of "Modern" Humans. Rebecca Rogers Ackermann et al. in *Evolutionary Biology*, Vol. 43, No. 1, pages 1–11; March 2016.

Did Our Species Evolve in Subdivided Populations across Africa, and Why Does It Matter? Eleanor M. L. Scerri et al. in *Trends in Ecology & Evolution*. Published online July 11, 2018.

About the Author

Kate Wong is a senior editor for evolution and ecology at Scientific American.

Losing Key DNA Made Us Modern Humans

By Philip L. Reno

When we visit a zoo and peer at our closest living relatives, the great apes, two things reliably captivate us. One: they look so very much like people. The expressive faces and the grasping hands of chimpanzees, bonobos, orangutans and gorillas are eerily similar to our own.

The other: these creatures are so clearly *not* us. Our upright walking, capacious and clever brains, and a list of other traits sharply set us apart. What were the key defining events in evolution that make us uniquely human? Why did they happen—and how? Anthropologists and evolutionary biologists have toiled at such questions for decades and increasingly are turning to modern genetic technologies to help crack the mystery. We have found that some of the most important human characteristics—features that set us apart from our closest relatives—may have come not from additions to our genes, as one might expect. Instead they have come out of losses: the disappearance of key stretches of DNA.

Several research laboratories, including mine, have traced some of this lost DNA across time, comparing human genomes with those of other mammals and even archaic humans: the Neandertals and our lesser known cousins, the Denisovans. We have learned that during the roughly eight million years since our lineage split from chimps, our ancestors' genomes were stripped of DNA "switches" that activate key genes during development. Neandertals share our loss, making it clear the vanishing act occurred early in our evolutionary path.

In fact, loss of these DNA sequences appears to be linked to quintessentially human traits: big brains, upright walking and our distinctive mating habits. (The last part of the project led me, in the course of my experiments, to learn a surprising amount about the structure of primate penises.)

Losers

I first developed a keen interest in human evolution during my Ph.D. years with noted anthropologist C. Owen Lovejoy of Kent State University, where I studied the difference in skeletons of males and females in extinct human relatives. I wanted to continue this kind of work to learn what, in our genes and developmental processes, had changed as humans progressed along our unusual evolutionary path. I was fortunate to obtain a postdoctoral position with David Kingsley of Stanford University, who was bearing down on just the kind of questions that fascinated me.

Among other work, Kingsley's lab had identified DNA changes involved in the evolution of stickleback fishes–including the deletion of a stretch of DNA in freshwater sticklebacks that, it turned out, caused the spiny pelvic fins to be lost in those species. That lost DNA piece contained a "switch" that was needed to activate a gene involved in pelvic spine development, at the right time and place.

If this kind of process had happened in sticklebacks, why not in human beings, too? It seemed reasonable to suppose that subtle changes in when and where genes are turned on during development might be one way our genome had evolved to generate our unique anatomy.

Inspired by that fishy example, we set out to see if we could find important switches that had disappeared in human beings over evolutionary time. Today's availability of completely sequenced human and ape genomes, as well as the computational tools needed to analyze them, made our experiments possible. A group of us in Kingsley's lab teamed up with Stanford computational scientist Gill Bejerano and then graduate student Cory McLean to plan the experiments.

Finding missing switches is not easy, because genomes are vast. Ours contains 3.2 billion bases (the individual letters of a DNA sequence), and about 100 million of these differ between humans and chimps. How could our experiment be done? To understand our approach, a bit of background is in order.

We know that in a creature's genome, stretches of DNA that are doing important jobs are preserved during evolution with high fidelity. We also know that the more closely related two species are, the more similar their genetic sequences will be. In the case of chimps and humans, for example, our genomes are 99 percent identical in the tiny portion—less than 1 percent—that carries instructions for making proteins. And they are 96 percent identical in the much larger portion of the genome that does not contain these protein-coding genes.

Searching the Junk Pile

We were interested in this much larger area—stretches that, in the past, were written off as "junk" DNA but are now known to be stuffed with switches that turn genes on and off. The work of these switches is crucial. Although pretty much all human body cells contain the same 20,000 or so genes, they are not all turned on everywhere or at all times and places. Only certain genes are needed to build a brain, for example, and others for bones or hair. Because chimps and humans, despite their differences, have the same basic bodily structure, it is not surprising that the vast, switch-containing terrain in our genomes has a lot of similarities.

The differences were what mattered to us. Specifically, we wanted to find sequences that had been preserved across evolutionary time in many species (indicating that the sequences were important) but were no longer present in humans. To do this, our computational genomics collaborators first compared the chimpanzee, macaque and mouse genomes. They pinpointed hundreds of DNA chunks that remained nearly unchanged among all three species. The next step was to scour this list to find chunks that did not exist in the human genome and thus had been lost sometime after our lineage diverged from the chimp's. We found more than 500.

Which of them to study? Because we wanted to find switches that might alter mammalian development, we focused on deletions near genes with known roles in that process. One of my colleagues pursued a deletion near a gene that regulates formation of neurons; another worked on a deletion near a gene involved in skeletal formation.

For my part, because of my interest in the evolution of the differences in male and female body forms, I was excited by a deletion near the gene for the androgen receptor. Androgens such as testosterone are hormones needed for the development of male-specific traits. Made in the testes, they circulate through the bloodstream. In response, cells that actively make androgen receptors will then follow a male pattern of development: formation of a penis instead of a clitoris, for example, or (later in life) beard growth and an enlarged larynx for a deep voice.

We needed, first, to test if those chunks of DNA really contained on-switches. To do this, we extracted them from both chimp and mouse DNA and attached them to a gene that turns cells blue—but only when that gene is activated. We injected this stitched-together piece of DNA into fertilized mouse eggs to see if any parts of the embryos were blue as they developed—indicating a functional switch in the piece of DNA—and, if so, where.

Male Turnoffs

My results were exciting: they really seemed to show that I was working with a true on-switch for the androgen receptor, one that human beings had shed. In mouse embryos, the genital tubercle (which develops into either a clitoris or penis) stained blue, as did the developing mammary glands and spots on the mouse face where sensory whiskers called vibrissae form. All these tissues are known to make the androgen receptor respond to testosterone. Looking more closely, I saw that the staining on the developing genitals was situated in places where small, tough protein spikes later form on the mouse penis.

Neither sensory whiskers or spiny penises are human features, of course. But they occur in many mammals, including mice, monkeys and chimps. It is also known that a loss of testosterone results in shorter whiskers in male rodents and a lack of penile spines in rodents and primates. Penile spines and whiskers might similarly disappear if a crucial DNA switch were lost and the androgen receptor were no longer made in these tissues.

Vahan B. Indjeian, then a postdoc in the lab, similarly found that his switch turned on the gene involved in skeletal growth—in developing hind limbs, specifically the toes of the foot. Toes two through five in humans are shorter than in apes and mice, alterations that improve the foot for upright walking.

It is easy to see how brain and bone switches fit into the pattern of human evolution. Loss of both appears linked to hallmarks of humanity: a big brain and walking on two legs. Loss of sensory whiskers is fairly easy to rationalize because we no longer root around in the dark with snouts to grub out food or capture prey but use hands, in daylight, to find nourishment. Despite their reduced importance, though, it is unclear how we would be better off without these whiskers.

Sensitive Relationships

The penile spine story is less intuitive, but it is potentially more powerful and also fits neatly into the adaptive history of our species. Loss of spines, we believe, is one of a suite of changes that together had far-reaching effects on our evolutionary path. Together these changes altered the ways we mate, the physical appearance of males and females, our relationships with one another and the ways we care for offspring.

Made of keratin, the same stuff as our fingernails, these spines occur in many mammals, including primates, rodents, cats, bats and opossums, and range from simple microscopic cones to large barbs and multipronged spikes. They may serve varied functions depending on the species: heightening stimulation, inducing ovulation, removing sperm deposited by other males, or irritating the vaginal lining to limit female interest in mating with others.

The copulation time of spine-sporting primates is remarkably brief: in the chimp, typically less than 10 seconds. And historical experiments in primates show that removal of penile spines can extend copulation by two thirds. From such observations we can surmise that loss of penile spines was one of the changes in humans that have made the sex act last longer, and thus be more intimate, compared with that of our spine-bearing forebears. That sounds pleasant, but it could also serve our species from an evolutionary perspective.

Our own reproductive strategy is unlike that of any apes, which all have intense male-male competition at their core. In chimps and bonobos, males compete to mate with as many fertile females as possible. They produce copious quantities of sperm (chimp testicles are three times larger than human ones), have penile spines and, like all male great apes and monkeys, have deadly, fanglike canines to discourage rivals. They leave rearing of offspring entirely to the female. Thus, for her, successful mating results in considerable commitment–gestating, nursing and rearing each infant to independence–and the female does not reproduce again until the weaning is completed.

Humans are different. They form fairly faithful pair bonds. Men often help to rear offspring, enabling earlier weaning and increasing reproductive rate. Male-male competition is not as intense. We believe that loss of penile spines went along with loss of other traits associated with fierce competition (such as dangerous canines) and gain of others that promote bonding and cooperation.

Bipedalism, as Lovejoy proposed, could be one of these features. Early male help probably initially took the form of procuring foods rich in fat and proteins, such as grubs, insects and small vertebrates, that required extensive search and transport. Males would need to travel far with hands free for carrying, which likely provided the initial selective advantage for walking on two legs.

Gene Loss and Feature Gains

And there is more. Cooperation and provisioning would also allow parents to rear dependent offspring for longer and thus lengthen the juvenile period after weaning. This would offer a longer time for learning and therefore enhance the usefulness of a large, agile brain–indeed, perhaps set the stage for its evolution.

In that sense, the individual stories of all three of our deletions are deeply intertwined.

When I came to Kingsley's lab, I did not anticipate the turn my work would take–that I would find myself poring over fusty 1940s texts on mammalian genital structure. My lab is continuing research into this and other genetic and developmental changes with big consequences: the evolutionary shaping of the delicate bones in the human wrist to perfect them for toolmaking.

There is much we may never know about all this distant history, no matter how keen we may be to find out. But even if we cannot be sure about the why of an evolutionary change, with the tools of modern molecular biology we can now tackle the how–a critical and fascinating question in its own right.

Referenced

Reexamining Human Origins in Light of *Ardipithecus ramidus*. C. Owen Lovejoy in *Science*, Vol. 326, pages 74–74e8; October 2, 2009.

Human-Specific Loss of Regulatory DNA and the Evolution of Human-Specific Traits. Cory Y. McLean et al. in *Nature*, Vol. 471, pages 216–219; March 10, 2011.

A Penile Spine/Vibrissa Enhancer Sequence Is Missing in Modern and Extinct Humans but Is Retained in Multiple Primates with Penile Spines and Sensory Vibrissae. Philip L. Reno et al. in *PLOS ONE*, Vol. 8, No. 12, Article No. e84258; December 19, 2013.

Genetic and Developmental Basis for Parallel Evolution and Its Significance for Hominoid Evolution. Philip L. Reno in *Evolutionary Anthropology: Issues, News, and Reviews*, Vol. 23, No. 5, pages 188–200; September/October 2014.

Evolving New Skeletal Traits by Cis-Regulatory Changes in Bone Morphogenetic Proteins. Vahan B. Indjeian et al. in *Cell*, Vol. 164, Nos. 1–2, pages 45–56; January 14, 2016.

About the Author

Philip L. Reno is an associate professor of biomedical sciences at the Philadelphia College of Osteopathic Medicine.

Ancient Girl Had Denisovan and Neandertal Parents

By Krystal D'Costa

There have been a ton of great discoveries this summer that enhance our understanding of our evolutionary history, including a study recently released in *Nature* confirming that two groups of our evolutionary cousins–Neanderthals and Denisovans–likely interbred more frequently than was previously known. The implications of this study have a direct bearing on us: modern humans carry genetic traces of both Neanderthal and Denisovan DNA and unraveling this complicated genetic heritage may allow us to better understand the social landscape of our evolutionary ancestors. Everything we know about the Denisovans comes from a small body of evidence consisting of a partial finger bone, two teeth, and a single toe recovered from the Denisova Cave in the Altai Mountains in Siberia. From these scarce human remains we've sequenced the Denisovan genome, but we have little else to help us understand who they were and how they lived. We haven't found any tools or artifacts that can be definitively linked to them.

The story we have put together has been largely thanks to genetics. We know they were a distinct ancestral species; they diverged from the Neanderthal line 400,000 years ago. They participated in one (or many) of the waves of migration out of Africa, but it's hard to pinpoint exactly when given the evidence we have. Their migrations would have occurred between 300,000 years ago, when Neanderthals began their migration, and 60,000 years ago when modern humans followed. And we know these groups did not keep to themselves: Denisovan DNA can be found in living humans from Asia (less than 1%) and Melanesia (up to 6%). In fact, modern Tibetans have a variation of a gene that regulates blood hemoglobin, which allows them to live in oxygen-thin places at high elevations. This gene can be traced to the Denisovans. European and Asian populations carry 1-2% of Neanderthal DNA and scientists believe that genetic inheritance had a large part to play in the adaptability of modern humans to a wide range of environments as these genes impact everything from blood clotting to depression and addiction to sun sensitivity. How these different groups of hominids interacted remains something that is less understood.

But with the recent news coming out of Denisova Cave, we may have another small piece of the puzzle. Researchers retrieved more than 2,000 bone fragments in 2008, including a tiny remnant of a "long bone" labeled Denisova 11. The thickness of the outer part of the bone fragment suggests that the bone belonged to a female of about 13 years old, while radiocarbon dating tells us she lived 50,000 –90,000 years ago. What is truly remarkable about this fragment, however, is that the mitochondrial DNA, which is inherited from the mother, resembled DNA from a Neanderthal found in Croatia (but not the Neanderthals previously identified within the Denisova cave). Her yDNA–the DNA inherited from her father–was Denisovan, although he seems to have had a touch of Neanderthal DNA in his heritage as well. She has been nicknamed Denny. From the long bone sample that represents her entire existence, 38.6% of the fragments collected carried alleles matching the Neanderthal genome while 42.3% carried alleles matching the Denisovan genome. She is physical proof that Neanderthals and Denisovans were interacting and interbreeding with each other.

Her genetic similarity with the Croatian Neanderthal gives us clues to a possible migration pattern. The Croatian Neanderthal died about 55,000 years ago, which is a more definite date than the age assigned to Denny, and the Neanderthal recovered from Denisova Cave is about 120,000 years old. Scientists propose that Denny's mother came from a group of Neanderthals that either traveled east to the Altai Mountains and partly replaced the local Neanderthals or a group the left the Altai mountains and traveled into Europe after she was born. In this scenario, the Neanderthals are roamers which fits with the fossil remains and genetic heritage that we have been able to find to date.

The work to arrive at understanding Denny's parentage warrants its own recognition. While the media celebrations the conclusion, the work that it takes to arrive at the "Aha!" moment isn't often acknowledged. This work began in 1984 with the first discovery of a tooth. In 2000, another tooth was found, and in 2008, a collection of 2,000 unidentified bone fragments were analyzed for signs for human proteins. The scientists revealed they had been able to date the fragment to 50,000 – 90,000 years ago using radiocarbon dating in 2016, and began to sequence the mitochondrial DNA to compare the data to other known sequences. This study provided evidence on the parentage of Denisova 11–although it does not delve too deeply into the possibility that the parents themselves were of mixed Neanderthal-Denisovan heritage. This represents a span of over three decades of work to unravel, unveil and identify a fragment of our evolutionary history.

We don't yet understand how the Denisovans and Neanderthals and modern humans interacted–whether these were peaceful meetings or not. And scientists say that there is yet unidentified ancient DNA in our lineage that does not belong to either the Denisovans or Neanderthals so there is more for us to learn about our genetic and social history. These findings do tell us that these meetings may have been more frequent than we understand–and the larger story continues to unfold.

Referenced

Slon, Viviane et. al. (2018) The genome of the offspring of a Neanderthal mother and a Denisovan father. *Nature* (561): 113-116.

About the Author

Krystal D'Costa is an anthropologist working in digital media in New York City.

The Fossil That Rewrote Human Prehistory

By Jason Heaton, Travis Rayne Pickering, Dominic Stratford

In August 1936, Robert Broom, a Scottish doctor with a keen interest in paleontology, visited a lime quarry in South Africa called Sterkfontein. In a guidebook at the time, the owner of the site, wrote, "Come to Sterkfontein and find the 'missing link.'" It would not be long before Broom did just that.

On Broom's third visit to Sterkfontein, the quarry's manager George Barlow presented him with a lump of calcified sediment in the shape of a brain, complete with convolutions and venous patterns. It was of modest size, but was certainly bigger than that of a monkey or other animal whose fossils were commonly found in the caves of the area. He soon located much of the cranium as well as many of its associated teeth and determined the pieces represented a fossil human called an ape-man.

At the time, the only other example of an ape-man was the "Taung Child" skull. Due to its developmentally young age, the scientific community had been reluctant to embrace the fossil as a legitimate human ancestor, because the bones of juvenile apes and humans look more alike than their adult counterparts.

Eighty years ago, on September 19, 1936, Broom published his findings, which would reshape our knowledge of our earliest ancestors. The fossils began to suggest that Africa was the ancestral homeland of our lineage, and not Europe or Asia as was previously believed. Now called the "Cradle of Humankind," the rolling hills between Johannesburg and Pretoria have since advanced our knowledge far beyond Broom's initial revelation and continue to further academic knowledge to this day.

The region attracted major attention long before the first human fossils were ever found there. In the 1890s, gold was discovered in the caves and later was mined for the tremendous lime resources also found there. Although the raw materials have been stripped, the fossils have proven to be the more precious resource.

In 1947, eight years after the end of the lime mining, Broom returned to Sterkfontein with zoologist John Robinson, searching strictly for fossils. Within three weeks, Broom and Robinson were rewarded with the recovery of an ape-man skull, nicknamed Mrs. Ples. Other findings quickly accrued, including a partial skeleton, the anatomy of which showed that although small-brained and apelike in many ways, the ape-men of nearly 3-million-years-ago were also upright, two-legged walkers, similar to modern humans.

By 1956, younger deposits were discovered at Sterkfontein by C. K. Brain, a geology student who also recognized primitive stone tools in these new sediments. Importantly, these tools were associated with fossils of more advanced species of our own genus, *Homo*.

After 10 years of inactivity at Sterkfontein, anatomist Phillip Tobias and his assistant Alun Hughes initiated systematic excavations at Sterkfontein in November 1966. It was not until 18 long months later that the first fossil human scraps were recovered. Over the next 25 years the two men would recover hundreds of fossils.

One of the most significant decisions they made was in 1978, when they began to investigate the deep underground portions of Sterkfontein, including an area called the Silberberg Grotto. Lime miners had been active in the grotto and left hundreds of blocks of calcified, fossil-rich sediment strewn across the area. Hughes collected the fossils and stored them in boxes to study later.

After Hughes died in 1991, paleontologist Ron Clarke took his place. Clarke went to the fossils that hadn't moved from the boxes for nearly 15 years, where he discovered a misidentified and previously unknown ape-man bone. He later discovered 12 bones of the foot and leg of a single ape-man.

Many bones within these South African caves found their way there through the action of carnivores who dragged animal carcasses to the caves to eat in seclusion. This messy process usually broke and scattered bones, covering them with tooth marks.

Since Clarke discovered bones in an entirely different state of preservation, he was confident that his ape-man had escaped being a carnivore's meal; indeed, he believed that there was a complete skeleton somewhere in the depths of the Silberberg Grotto.

In June of 1997, two of Clarke's assistants, Nkwane Molefe and Stephen Motsumi, were tasked with the impossible: trying to find a tibia where the rest of Clarke's ape-man likely rested. He believed that since it was likely broken during the mining activities 65 years prior, that the remaining bone might still be visible.

Despite the massive, dank and dark surroundings of the Silberberg Grotto, Molefe and Motsumi found the broken tibia after just two days of searching, armed only with handheld lamps.

Over the next several years of extraction, Clarke's prediction of an entire ape-man skeleton was confirmed. What was nicknamed "Little Foot" by Tobias, has been lifted from the depths and is being prepared and described by Clarke. Dating techniques estimate "Little Foot" to be 3.7 million years old, more than a million years older than the ape-men fossils first found by Broom and Robinson decades before.

When finally fully described, "Little Foot" will be an anthropological "Rosetta Stone," allowing other isolated and broken fragments to be better understood when compared to this complete skeleton.

After 80 years, we're honored to collaborate with Clarke in continuing his work at this iconic site. As we move forward with our exploration of the caves, one of our primary goals is to integrate excavation data from the last 50 years with high-resolution stratigraphic, sedimentological and geochemical information.

This evidence will further reveal the "big picture" of Sterkfontein's history and our own evolutionary past, and will hopefully prove part of the proud legacy of Robert Broom's astonishing discoveries.

The views expressed are those of the author(s) and are not necessarily those of Scientific American.

About the Authors

Jason Heaton is associate professor of biology at Birmingham-Southern College

Travis Rayne Pickering is professor of anthropology at the University of Wisconsin-Madison

Dominic Stratford is senior lecturer of geoarchaeology at the University of the Witwatersrand, South Africa

Nobel Winner Svante Pääbo Discovered the Neandertal in Our Genes

By Daniela Mocker

Scientists have always been fascinated by the question of human origins: When and where did modern humans–*Homo sapiens*–first appear? What distinguishes us from other members of the genus *Homo* and enabled us to develop such unprecedented culture and society?

Indeed, hardly any question fascinates humanity as much as our own roots. For thousands of years, clerics, scholars and philosophers have been racking their brains about where we come from, who are we and where are we going. The French painter Paul Gauguin was so captivated by that line of inquiry that he even dedicated a painting so named in the 19th century. The work, which deals with both the meaning and the transience of life, remains his most famous.

We have come a lot closer to answering these big questions thanks in part to the work of the paleogeneticist Svante Pääbo. He achieved what others had long thought impossible: he decoded the genome of Neandertals, a relative of modern humans who went extinct around 30,000 years ago. The Nobel Assembly at the Karolinska Institute in Stockholm honored him this year with the Nobel Prize in Medicine or Physiology for his contribution to the study of human evolution.

Ancient DNA is Difficult to Analyze

When Pääbo began working with ancient DNA in the 1980s, the discovery of Neandertals was long a thing of the past. The first fossils of early humans had already been unearthed in the mid-19th century. At first glance this species seemed to be more closely related to modern humans than almost any other. But just how Neandertals were related to *Homo sapiens* was a subject of repeated controversy in the decades following the discovery. For example, some wondered whether Neandertals could possibly have been an ancestor of modern humans–a hypothesis that most experts have since rejected.

Genetic data could undoubtedly shed light on the connection between modern humans and Neandertals. Analyzing the genome of a living species was one thing, but obtaining genetic samples of a species extinct for tens of thousands of years was quite another. Over time, DNA changes chemically and gradually breaks down into short fragments. So after thousands of years, only traces of it remain among bone samples, and those traces are usually heavily contaminated with foreign DNA.

Journey to the Neandertal

That didn't deter Pääbo. As early as 1984, while doing his doctorate at Uppsala University, he caused a small sensation when he managed to isolate DNA from the cells of a 2,400-year-old Egyptian mummy for the first time. Fearing that his doctoral supervisor would forbid him from doing the research, he secretly carried out his studies at night and on weekends, as he later explained. But by the time the journal *Nature* picked up the results, everyone was talking about his work. At the time it was the only paper published on DNA from fossil tissues.

Soon after, Pääbo joined Allan Wilson's group at the University of California, Berkeley. Here he dealt, among other things, with the genome of extinct animals such as mammoths and cave bears. But Neandertals were always among his chief interests, Pääbo told *Spektrum der Wissenschaft* in 2008. Ultimately, he wanted to find out what makes humans human, and which genetic changes contributed to human evolution.

In 1990 he continued this research at the University of Munich. There he decided to focus first on mitochondrial DNA, copies of which are present in a significantly higher number inside the cell nucleus compared to DNA. In 1997 he finally succeeded in isolating the genetic material from an approximately 40,000-year-old Neanderthal bone that was part of a Neandertal skeleton found near Düsseldorf in the 1850s. This was the first time the world had access to a piece of Neandertal genome.

Comparisons with the mitochondrial DNA of modern humans and chimpanzees soon showed that the Neandertals differed genetically from both species: *Homo sapiens* and *Homo neanderthalensis* did not share more than 10 percent of their genes.

Genes in Common

In contrast to the DNA from the cell nucleus, the mitochondrial genome is small. It contains only a fraction of all the genes that a living being possesses and is therefore of limited usefulness. Further progress in the field therefore depended on obtaining the complete Neandertal genome. In order to clear the last hurdle, Pääbo, then the newly appointed director of the recently founded Max Planck Institute for Evolutionary Anthropology in Leipzig, Germany, continued to refine his methods over the coming years. In 2010 he finally made his breakthrough and was able to present the world with the first version of a fully sequenced Neandertal genome.

Pääbo and his team's research indicated that the last common ancestor of modern humans and Neandertals must have lived around 800,000 years ago. They also proved gene flow from Neandertals to modern humans: both species apparently interbred in the millennia that they lived simultaneously on earth, primarily in Europe and Asia, where the human genomes sequenced contain 1 to 4 percent Neandertal genes.

Pääbo and his team also sequenced the genome of Denisova, a hominin whose fossils were found in 2008 in the Denisova Cave in the Altai Mountains in Siberia. The group was not only able to show that the Denisova was a new, previously unknown early human species, but also that the Denisova maintained close contact with ancestors of modern humans; in some regions of Southeast Asia, humans share up to 6 percent of their genes with the extinct Denisovans.

The Circle Closes

Today, Pääbo is rightly regarded as one of the founders of paleogenetics. "His work has revolutionized our understanding of the evolutionary history of modern humans," stated Martin Stratmann, president of the Max Planck Society, in a press release. Chris Stringer of the Natural History Museum in London offered similar praise; that Pääbo is now receiving the Nobel Prize is great news, the paleoanthropologist told *Nature*.

Pääbo's work has not only shed new light on our past. Further studies indicate that our Neandertal heritage also influences our present. For example, some of the genes seem to have an impact on how the immune system reacts to various pathogens. In 2021, Pääbo and his team made headlines when they reported that people with a specific Neandertal variant on the third chromosome were at a higher risk of developing severe COVID-19.

The answers to the two questions of where we come from and where we are going might end up being more similar than we thought.

About the Author

Daniela Mocker is deputy editor in chief of Spektrum.de.

Piltdown Man Came from *The Lost World*... Well, No, It Didn't

By Darren Naish

In 1908, amateur geologist and solicitor Charles Dawson claimed the discovery of a new and exciting fossil that, so it was thought, shed substantial light on the ancestry of humans. Dubbed Piltdown man, and technically named *Eoanthropus dawsoni*, it was (... *spoiler*...) eventually shown to be a hoax–one of the most nefarious, infamous and successful scientific hoaxes of all time.

Piltdown man never was accepted with open arms by the scientific community as a whole. On the contrary, experts in the UK, USA and continental Europe all expressed considerable doubt about the homogeneity of the material. Anyway, there are a great many stories attached to the Piltdown man arc, and in this article I'm going to cover another one.

Regular Tet Zoo readers might know that I have a long-standing research interest in the fossil dinosaurs (and other tetrapods) of the Lower Cretaceous English rock unit known as the Wealden Supergroup. The Wealden is one of the most famous rock units in the world and is formed of sediments deposited in both the Wessex Basin (corresponding to the Isle of Wight) and the Weald Basin (corresponding to the Weald of south-eastern mainland England). But the Weald doesn't just yield these Cretaceous, Wealden fossils. Far younger ones, dating to the Pleistocene, are preserved in the younger sediments of the region, and among them were, supposedly, the remains of Piltdown man and a contemporaneous fauna of proboscideans and other mammals.

But how is this provenance-based data relevant to the hoax?

In 1912, Arthur Conan Doyle published his novel *The Lost World*. The story's general theme is well known, as is the fact that Doyle essentially single-handedly invented what is today a mainstream sci-fi trope. Far less well known is the claim that Maple White Land,

The Lost World's fictitious Brazilian plateau, was based on the Weald. At least, this is what researchers John Winslow and Alfred Meyer proposed in 1983, this being one small aspect of a far grander story in which the perpetration of the Piltdown hoax was pinned on Doyle (Winslow & Meyer 1983). Doyle lived only about 11 km from Barkham Manor (the Piltdown man discovery site), visited the excavations at least once, and was extremely knowledgeable as goes anatomy, geology, palaeontology, and the science and art of sleuthing and hoaxing. This is the man who invented Sherlock freaking Holmes. Could, Winslow and Meyer asked, Doyle have been behind the Piltdown hoax?

No. Not only was Winslow and Meyer's case wholly circumstantial and involved a great many speculations and guesses (*maybe* Doyle did this, *maybe* he did that), pointing the finger at Doyle ignores his upstanding character, strong moral conviction, and packed schedule during the years concerned. Sure, we know that Doyle visited Barkham Manor once, but the planted fossils that were found there were discovered on *over twenty* separate occasions. A vague idea that Doyle's strong interest in spiritualism instilled in him a desire to belittle or ruin the "realists" of the day (Winslow & Meyer 1983) is also erroneous, since Doyle didn't properly develop this belief until 1916 (it was mostly catalysed by the events of World War I) and it cannot be linked with any hypothetical involvement in the Piltdown affair. Winslow & Meyer (1983), incidentally, weren't the only authors to propose Doyle as the hoaxer, but this idea has always come under heavy and appropriate criticism when put forward.

Also part of Winslow and Meyer's case was their claim that Doyle's map of Maple White Land is (cough) *clearly* based on the Weald (Winslow & Meyer 1983). Maple White Land had a lake in the middle, a river running north-south in its southern half, an "Iguanodon glade" to the east of the river, a place where giant deer were seen in the west, a precarious "pinnacle of ascent" in the south, and a place where a battle occurred in the east. In the Weald, a rock group known as the Hastings Group (originally, and traditionally, the Hastings Sands) forms (so claimed Winslow and Meyer) a vaguely lake-shaped outcrop in the centre of the region, the River Ouse runs north-south, Lewes (where *Iguanodon* was first discovered) is close by, Harting Down is in the west ("Harting" = obvious link with deer), the precarious Beachy Head is in the south, and the town of... *Battle* is over to the east (sort of).

In *The Lost World*, Malone (the main character) encounters an ape-man, and does so near the Iguanodon glade (Doyle 1912). When we compare the map of Maple White Land with that of the Weald, we see (so claimed Winslow and Meyer) that this spot corresponds approximately with the real-life location of Piltdown. Was Doyle's ape-man a heavy-handed reference to Piltdown man? Winslow and Meyer thought so, but what they missed is that the ape-man in *The Lost World* is categorically unlike Piltdown man, a point emphasised by John Walsh in his critique of Winslow and Meyer's case (Walsh 1996). Piltdown man was supposed to have a big, human-like brain, flattened brow region, and an "ape-like" jaw (albeit with straight canines far smaller than those associated with "apes"). But Doyle's ape-man is very different, with a thick, heavy brow and prominent, curved canines (Doyle 1912).

As if it's not already obvious, those supposed similarities between Maple White Land and the Weald are all terribly vague and not especially compelling–the locations don't really match at all and the real-life geographical features that Winslow pointed to are not similar to the features of Maple White Land (Walsh 1996). In any case, we have quite good reasons for thinking that Doyle invented Maple White Land after learning about some key localities in South America, most notably the Huanchaca Plateau in Bolivia. Winslow and Meyer's idea was discussed favourably (as if it were likely true) in Spencer Lucas' *Dinosaurs The Textbook* (Lucas 1994), though Winslow and Meyer are neither mentioned nor cited in that book. No comment.

In the end, this whole proposal of a link between Piltdown man and a fictional land full of dinosaurs and pterosaurs never did warrant serious consideration, nor was there ever a good case to be made for Doyle being the hoaxer.

Referenced

Collins, J. 1981. *The Lost World*. Ladybird Books, Loughborough.

Doyle, A. C. 1912. *The Lost World*. Hodder & Stoughton, London.

Lucas, S. 1994. *Dinosaurs The Textbook*. Wm. C. Brown Publishers, Dubuque, Iowa.

Walsh, J. E. 1996. *Unravelling Piltdown*. Random House, New York.

Winslow, J. & Meyer, A. 1983. The perpetrator at Piltdown. *Science* 83 September 1983, 33-43.

About the Author

Darren Naish is a science writer, technical editor and palaeozoologist (affiliated with the University of Southampton, UK). He mostly works on Cretaceous dinosaurs and pterosaurs but has an avid interest in all things tetrapod. His publications can be downloaded at darrennaish.wordpress.com. He has been blogging at Tetrapod Zoology *since 2006.*

Section 2: What Makes Us Human?

What Makes the Human Foot Unique?

By Krystal D'Costa

Our feet stand us up. The bones that make up the feet represent a quarter of the human skeleton, and yet, despite comprising such a large percentage of the body, they have largely eluded us in the fossil record until recently. This is frustrating because it's clear that this story—the evolution of the human foot—has captivated us for hundreds of years. It is after all linked to the pivotal development of bipedalism in our history. Understanding differences between our feet and those of other apes (both ancestral and contemporary), can give us clues into the changes that were necessary for bipedalism—and perhaps for bipedalism itself. What has emerged is a story of diversity in locomotion that supports a case for mosaic evolution making the story of the foot overall (not just ours) a remarkable one.

A recent review article from researchers Ellison McNutt and colleagues tracks the literature on the evolution of the human foot. The quest to know ourselves begins in 1699 with an anatomical assessment of modern chimpanzees by Edward Tyson who labeled them quadrumanous, meaning all of their appendages were adapted to function as hands. In 1863 Thomas H. Huxley would make comparisons to gorilla feet and call out that while they were also inverted and possessed grasping tendencies, they also shared muscular similarities with the human foot. In 1935 anatomy professor Dudley Morton proposed the modern human foot is the result of two distinct transitions. In the first instance, the foot would have possessed more "ape-like" qualities with greater grasping abilities and flexibility, and notably an elongated midfoot region. In later stages, the foot would have moved away from these traits, although it may have retained the "grasping" ability with the big toe.

These ideas were fine, but what we needed were fossils. The discovery of OH 8 in 1960 by the Leakey team in Olduvai Gorge propelled us forward. OH 8 refers to Olduvai Hominid number 8 and dates to about 1.8 million years old. It belonged to a member of

Homo habilis family and includes the the left tarsal and metatarsal bones–the tarsals are a series of bones that comprise the plane of the foot leading to the toes–but no actual toes. Taken together with the discovery of Lucy, as well as the Laetoli footprints, OH 8 served the story that the human foot was adapted from the arboreal chimpanzee foot. However, in 1995, scientists proposed that the anatomy of the ankle joint and heel (the hindfoot) existed before the anatomy of the human forefoot as it pertains to bipedalism. This was based on the discovery of "Little Foot," an almost complete *Australopithecus* fossil skeleton recovered from Sterkfontein, South Africa dating to 3.3 million years ago, which exhibited similar hindfoot traits. Scientists believed that the foot of *Australopithecus* was adapted for bipedalism but it also allowed this early human ancestor to take refuge in the trees if needed. In piecing together these discoveries, it became clear that the evolutionary story of the human foot wouldn't be explained linearly. The human foot evolved independently of other developments within human evolution and at different rates between species.

One of the things we can say with certainty is that the modern human foot did not evolve from the chimpanzee foot. As reasonable as it may seem to draw comparisons between the two, the clear divergence between the genera from a last common ancestor (LCA) means that hominins and panins evolved feet to suit their needs. A major difference between the two stems from flexibility. The former's foot is adapted for a stiff push-off which is necessary for bipedal locomotion. The latter's feet maintains greater flexibility overall and grasping abilities that enable climbing trees as well quadrupedalism on the ground. Close anatomical analysis reveals that many of the differences between the two orient around the stiffness of one versus the flexibility of the other with robust versus gracile features that support different musculature and movement. For example, the big toe of humans is thick in comparison to that of a chimpanzee, and is aligned with the other toes, which allows the foot to push off the ground. This "big toe" is not only more gracile in chimpanzees, but it curves toward the other toes enabling a greater flexing motion. These characteristics are true of the toes in general also. In humans these bones are more robust and may help absorb some of the pressure of the push-off, while in chimpanzees these bones are extended and curved with higher degrees of flexibility.

The chimpanzee foot most likely contains derived elements that were adapted to support their arboreal lifestyle. If we want to unlock the "ancestral foot," the modern human foot may hold clues. We haven't yet identified the last common ancestor we shared with chimpanzee, but we do have some very old hominid fossils, such as *Pierolapithecus catalaunicus* (11.9 million years old) and hominin fossils like *Ardipithecus ramidus* (4.4 million years old). The latter is the oldest hominin fossil we have with a relatively complete foot. Between these bookends and other Miocene apes, we can do the same thing that Morton did and generate a proposal for the LCA. We can predict that it may have possessed gracile features to facilitate grasping and flexibility. It would have been inverted, but it may also have passed a stiffer, more robust midfoot to allow for terrestrial activities.

Following the transition from *Australopithecus* to *Homo*, toes decreased in length and curvature, the ankle and corresponding musculature reduced in size, and full foot arches emerged. The big toe shifted to align with the other toes rather than curving inward enabling a more efficient push-off for bipedalism. There are some exceptions to these developments. In *Homo naledi*, for example, the toes are more curved than they are in the *Homo* genus overall. And *Homo floriensis* has an elongated forefoot, which most closely resembles that of bonobos. These kinds of variations aren't unusual; the heel bones of modern great apes vary between species. These cases illustrate a diversity in foot evolution and locomotion, which with time may offer greater contextual clues about the lives of these groups.

The story of the human foot is still unfolding. It is unique because it is best suited to our style of bipedal locomotion. The variations that scientists have found in foot bones for australopiths suggest there was variation in how they walked even among themselves, which is true of humans today: we have different stride lengths and different ways of coming down on our feet. Some have a more forceful step than others, to say nothing of how the feet of dancers are changed with years of training. Our story has the added complexity of the impact of habitual shoe wearing. It has changed the way we walk and undoubted changed the morphology of our feet. It will need to account for prosthetics and accessibility options. The story, while incomplete, remains no less fascinating that it was hundreds of years ago when all we had was a comparative assessment.

Referenced

McNutt EJ, Zipfel B, DeSilva JM. The evolution of the human foot. Evol Anthropol. 2018;1–21.

About the Author

Krystal D'Costa is an anthropologist working in digital media in New York City.

What Made Us Unique

By Kevin Laland

Our uniqueness has to do with a capacity to teach skills to others over the generations with enough precision for building skyscrapers or going to the moon.

Most people on this planet blithely assume, largely without any valid scientific rationale, that humans are special creatures, distinct from other animals. Curiously, the scientists best qualified to evaluate this claim have often appeared reticent to acknowledge the uniqueness of *Homo sapiens*, perhaps for fear of reinforcing the idea of human exceptionalism put forward in religious doctrines. Yet hard scientific data have been amassed across fields ranging from ecology to cognitive psychology affirming that humans truly are a remarkable species.

The density of human populations far exceeds what would be typical for an animal of our size. We live across an extraordinary geographical range and control unprecedented flows of energy and matter: our global impact is beyond question. When one also considers our intelligence, powers of communication, capacity for knowledge acquisition and sharing–along with magnificent works of art, architecture and music we create–humans genuinely do stand out as a very different kind of animal. Our culture seems to separate us from the rest of nature, and yet that culture, too, must be a product of evolution.

The challenge of providing a satisfactory scientific explanation for the evolution of our species' cognitive abilities and their expression in our culture is what I call "Darwin's Unfinished Symphony." That is because Charles Darwin began the investigation of these topics some 150 years ago, but as he himself confessed, his understanding of how we evolved these attributes was in his own words "imperfect" and "fragmentary." Fortunately, other scientists have taken up the baton, and there is an increasing feeling among those of us who conduct research in this field that we are closing in on an answer.

The emerging consensus is that humanity's accomplishments derive from an ability to acquire knowledge and skills from other people. Individuals then build iteratively on that reservoir of pooled knowledge over long periods. This communal store of experience enables creation of ever more efficient and diverse solutions to life's challenges. It was not our large brains, intelligence or language that gave us culture but rather our culture that gave us large brains, intelligence and language. For our species and perhaps a small number of other species, too, culture transformed the evolutionary process.

The term "culture" implies fashion or haute cuisine, but boiled down to its scientific essence, culture comprises behavior patterns shared by members of a community that rely on socially transmitted information. Whether we consider automobile designs, popular music styles, scientific theories or the foraging of small-scale societies, all evolve through endless rounds of innovations that add incremental refinements to an initial baseline of knowledge. Perpetual, relentless copying and innovation–that is the secret of our species' success.

Animal Talents

Comparing humans with other animals allows scientists to determine the ways in which we excel, the qualities we share with other species and when particular traits evolved. A first step to understanding how humans got to be so different, then, is to take this comparative perspective and investigate the social learning and innovation of other creatures, a search that leads ultimately to the subtle but critical differences that make us unique.

Many animals copy the behavior of other individuals and in this way learn about diet, feeding techniques, predator avoidance, or calls and songs. The distinctive tool-using traditions of different populations of chimpanzees throughout Africa is a famous example. In each community, youngsters learn the local behavior–be it cracking open nuts with a stone hammer or fishing for ants with a stick–by copying more experienced individuals. But social learning is not restricted to primates, large-brained animals or even vertebrates.

Thousands of experimental studies have demonstrated copying of behavior in hundreds of species of mammals, birds, fishes and insects. Experiments even show that young female fruit flies select as mates males that older females have chosen.

A diverse range of behaviors are learned socially. Dolphins possess traditions for foraging using sea sponges to flush out fish hiding on the ocean floor. Killer whales have seal-hunting traditions, including the practice of knocking seals off ice floes by charging toward them in unison and creating a giant wave. Even chickens acquire cannibalistic tendencies through social learning from other chickens. Most of the knowledge transmitted through animal populations concerns food—what to eat and where to find it—but there are also extraordinary social conventions. One troop of capuchin monkeys in Costa Rica has devised the bizarre habit of inserting fingers into the eye sockets or nostrils of other monkeys or hands into their mouths, sitting together in this manner for long periods and gently swaying—conventions that are thought to test the strength of social bonds.

Animals also "innovate." When prompted to name an innovation, we might think of the invention of penicillin by Alexander Fleming or the construction of the World Wide Web by Tim Berners-Lee. The animal equivalents are no less fascinating. My favorite concerns a young chimpanzee called Mike, whom primatologist Jane Goodall observed devising a noisy dominance display that involved banging two empty kerosene cans together. This exhibition thoroughly intimidated Mike's rivals and led to him shooting up the social rankings to become alpha male in record time. Then there is the invention by Japanese carrion crows of using cars to crack open nuts. Walnuts shells are too tough for crows to crack in their beaks, but they nonetheless feed on these nuts by placing them in the road for cars to run over, returning to retrieve their treats when the lights turn red. And a group of starlings—birds famously fond of shiny objects used as nest decorations—started raiding a coin machine at a car wash in Fredericksburg, Va., and made off with, quite literally, hundreds of dollars in quarters.

Such stories are more than just enchanting snippets of natural history. Comparative analyses reveal intriguing patterns in the social learning and innovation exhibited by animals. The most significant of these discoveries finds that innovative species, as well as animals most reliant on copying, possess unusually large brains (both in absolute terms and relative to body size). The correlation between rates of innovation and brain size was initially observed in birds, but this research has since been replicated in primates. These findings support a hypothesis known as cultural drive, first proposed by University of California, Berkeley, biochemist Allan C. Wilson in the 1980s.

Wilson argued that the ability to solve problems or to copy the innovations of others would give individuals an edge in the struggle to survive. Assuming these abilities had some basis in neurobiology, they would generate natural selection favoring ever larger brains—a runaway process culminating in the huge organs that orchestrate humans' unbounded creativity and all-encompassing culture.

Initially scientists were skeptical of Wilson's argument. If fruit flies, with their tiny brains, could copy perfectly well, then why should selection for more and more copying generate the proportionately gigantic brains seen in primates? This conundrum endured for years, until an answer arose from an unexpected source.

Copycats

The Social Learning Strategies Tournament was a competition that my colleagues and I organized that was designed to work out the best way to learn in a complex, changing environment. We envisaged a hypothetical world in which individuals—or agents as they are called—could perform a large number of possible behaviors, each with its own characteristic payoff that changed over time. The challenge was to work out which actions would give the best returns and to track how these changed. Individuals could either learn a new behavior or perform a previously learned one, and learning could occur through trial-and-error or through copying other individuals. Rather than trying to solve the puzzle ourselves, we described the problem and specified a set of rules, inviting anyone interested to have a go at solving it. All the entries–submitted as software code that specified how the agents should behave–competed against one another in a computer simulation, and the best performer won a €10,000 prize. The results were highly instructive. We found a strong positive relation between how well an entry performed and how well it required agents to learn socially. The winning entry did not require agents to learn often, but when they did, it was almost always through copying, which was always performed accurately and efficiently.

The tournament taught us how to interpret the positive relation between social learning and brain size observed in primates. The results suggested that natural selection does not favor more and more social learning but rather a tendency toward better and better social learning. Animals do not need a big brain to copy, but they do need a big brain to copy well.

This insight stimulated research into the empirical basis of the cultural drive hypothesis. It led to the expectation that natural selection ought to favor anatomical structures or functional capabilities in the primate brain that promote accurate, efficient copying. Examples might include better visual perception if that allows copying over greater distances or imitating fine-motor actions. In addition, selection should foster greater connections between perceptual and motor structures in the brain, helping individuals to translate the sight of others performing a skill into their producing a matching performance by moving their body in a corresponding way.

The same cultural drive hypothesis also predicted that selection for improved social learning should have influenced other aspects of social behavior and life history, including living in social groups and using tools. The reasoning was that the bigger the group and the more time spent in the company of others, the greater the opportunities for effective social learning. Through copying, monkeys and apes acquire diverse foraging skills ranging from extractive foraging methods such as digging grubs out of bark to sophisticated tool-using techniques such as fishing for termites with sticks. If social learning is what allows primates to pick up difficult-to-learn but productive food-procurement methods, any species proficient in social learning should show elevated levels of extractive foraging and tool use. They should possess a richer diet and have longer lives, if that gives more time for learning new skills and passing them on to descendants. In sum, cultural drive predicts that rates of social learning will correlate not only with brain size but also with a host of measures related to cognitive performance.

Rigorous comparative analyses have borne out these predictions. Those primates that excel at social learning and innovation are the same species that have the most diverse diets, use tools and extractive foraging, and exhibit the most complex social behavior. In fact, statistical analyses suggest that these abilities vary in lockstep so tightly that one can align primates along a single dimension of general cognitive performance, which we call primate intelligence (loosely analogous to IQ in humans).

Chimpanzees and orangutans excel in all these performance measures and have high primate intelligence, whereas some nocturnal prosimians are poor at most of them and have a lower metric. The strong correlations between primate intelligence and both brain size measures and performance in laboratory tests of learning and cognition validate the use of the metric as a measure of intelligence. The interpretation also fits with neuroscientific analyses showing that the size of individual brain components can be accurately predicted with knowledge of overall brain size. Associated with the evolution of large primate brains are bigger and better-connected regions—neocortices and cerebellums—that allow executive control of actions and increased cortical projections to the motor neurons of the limbs, facilitating controlled and precise movements. This helps us to understand why big-brained animals show complex cognition and tool use.

Plotting the intelligence measure on a primate family tree reveals evolution for higher intelligence taking place independently in four distinct primate groups: the capuchins, macaques, baboons and great apes—precisely those species renowned for their social learning and traditions. This finding is exactly the pattern expected if cultural processes really were driving the evolution of brain and cognition. Further analyses, using better data and cutting-edge statistical methods, reinforce these conclusions, as do models that make quantitative predictions for brain and body size based on estimates of the brain's metabolic costs.

Cultural drive is not the only cause of primate brain evolution: diet and sociality are also important because fruit-eating primates and those living in large, complex groups possess large brains. It is difficult, however, to escape the conclusion that high intelligence and longer lives co-evolved in some primates because their cultural capabilities allowed them to exploit high-quality but difficult-to-access food resources, with the nutrients gleaned "paying" for brain growth. Brains are energetically costly organs, and social learning is paramount to animals gathering the resources necessary to grow and maintain a large brain efficiently.

No Chimp Mobiles

Why, then, don't other primates have complex culture like us? Why haven't chimpanzees sequenced genomes or built space rockets? Mathematical theory has provided some answers. The secret comes down to the fidelity of information transmission from one member of a species to another, the accuracy with which learned information passes between transmitter and receiver. The size of a species' cultural repertoire and how long cultural traits persist in a population both increase exponentially with transmission fidelity. Above a certain threshold, culture begins to ratchet up in complexity and diversity. Without accurate transmission, cumulative culture is impossible. But once a given threshold is surpassed, even modest amounts of novel invention and refinement lead rapidly to massive cultural change. Humans are the only living species to have passed this threshold.

Our ancestors achieved high-fidelity transmission through teaching—behavior that functions to facilitate a pupil's learning.

Whereas copying is widespread in nature, teaching is rare, and yet teaching is universal in human societies once the many subtle forms this practice takes are recognized. Mathematical analyses reveal tough conditions that must be met for teaching to evolve, but they show that cumulative culture relaxes these conditions. The modeling implies that teaching and cumulative culture co-evolved in our ancestors, creating for the first time in the history of life on our planet a species whose members taught their relatives a broad range of skills, perhaps cemented through goal-oriented "deliberate" practice.

The teaching of cultural knowledge by hominins (humans and their extinct close relatives) included foraging, food processing, learned calls, toolmaking, and so forth and provided the context in which language first appeared. Why our ancestors alone evolved language is one of the great unresolved questions. One possibility is that language developed to reduce the costs, increase the accuracy and expand the domains of teaching. Human language may be unique, at least among extant species, because only humans constructed a sufficiently diverse and dynamic cultural world that demanded talking about. This explanation has the advantage that it accounts for many of the characteristic properties of language, including its distinctiveness, its power of generalization and why it is learned.

Language began as just a handful of shared symbols. But once started, the use of protolanguage imposed selection on hominin brains for language-learning skills and on languages themselves to favor easy-to-learn structures. That our ancestors' cultural activities imposed selection on their bodies and minds–a process known as gene culture co-evolution–is now well supported. Theoretical, anthropological and genomic analyses all demonstrate how socially transmitted knowledge, including that expressed in the manufacture and use of tools, generated natural selection that transformed human anatomy and cognition. This evolutionary feedback shaped the emergence of the modern human mind, generating an evolved psychology that spurred a motivation to teach, speak, imitate, emulate, and share the goals and intentions of others. It also produced enhanced learning and computational abilities. These capabilities evolved with cumulative culture because they enhance the fidelity of information transmission.

Teaching and language were evolutionary game changers for our lineage. Large-scale cooperation arose in human societies because of our uniquely potent capacities for social learning and teaching, as theoretical and experimental data attest. Culture took human populations down novel evolutionary pathways, both by creating conditions that promoted established mechanisms for cooperation witnessed in other animals (such as helping those that reciprocate) and by generating novel cooperative mechanisms not seen elsewhere. Cultural group selection—practices that help a group cooperate and compete with other groups (forming an army or building an irrigation system)—spread as they proved their worth.

Culture provided our ancestors with food-procurement and survival tricks, and as each new invention arose, a given population was able to exploit its environment more efficiently. This occurrence fueled not only brain expansion but population growth as well. Increases in both human numbers and societal complexity followed our domestication of plants and animals. Agriculture freed societies from the constraints that the peripatetic lives of hunter-gatherers imposed on population size and any inclinations to create new technologies. In the absence of this constraint, agricultural societies flourished, both because they outgrew hunter-gatherer communities through allowing an increase in the carrying capacity of a particular area for food production and because agriculture triggered a raft of associated innovations that dramatically changed human society. In the larger societies supported by increasing farming yields, beneficial innovations were more likely to spread and be retained. Agriculture precipitated a revolution not only by triggering the invention of related technologies—ploughs or irrigation technology, among others—but also by spawning entirely unanticipated initiatives, such as the wheel, city-states and religions.

The emerging picture of human cognitive evolution suggests that we are largely creatures of our own making. The distinctive features of humanity—our intelligence, creativity, language, as well as our ecological and demographic success–are either evolutionary adaptations to our ancestors' own cultural activities or direct consequences of those adaptations. For our species' evolution, cultural inheritance appears every bit as important as genetic inheritance.

We tend to think of evolution through natural selection as a process in which changes in the external environment, such as predators, climate or disease, trigger evolutionary refinements in an organism's traits. Yet the human mind did not evolve in this straightforward way. Rather our mental abilities arose through a convoluted, reciprocal process in which our ancestors constantly constructed niches (aspects of their physical and social environments) that fed back to impose selection on their bodies and minds, in endless cycles. Scientists can now comprehend the divergence of humans from other primates as reflecting the operation of a broad array of feedback mechanisms in the hominin lineage. Similar to a self-sustaining chemical reaction, a runaway process ensued that propelled human cognition and culture forward. Humanity's place in the evolutionary tree of life is beyond question. But our ability to think, learn, communicate and control our environment makes humanity genuinely different from all other animals.

A Visit From E.T.

Imagine an extraterrestrial intelligence studying Earth's biosphere. Which of all the species would it identify as differing from the rest? The answer is humanity. Here are a few reasons:

- **Population size.** Our numbers are out of kilter with global patterns for vertebrate populations. There are several orders of magnitude more humans than expected for a mammal of our size.
- **Ecological range.** Our species distribution is extraordinary. Humans have colonized virtually every region of the terrestrial globe.

- **Environmental regulation.** Humans control vast and diverse flows of energy and matter on unprecedented scales.
- **Global impact.** Human activities threaten and are driving extinct unmatched numbers of species while eliciting strong evolutionary change across the biosphere.
- **Cognition, communication and intelligence.** Experiments demonstrate superior performance by humans across diverse tests of learning and cognition. Human language is infinitely flexible, unlike the communication of other animals.
- **Knowledge acquisition and sharing.** Humans acquire, share and store information on never-before-seen scales and build on their pooled cultural knowledge cumulatively from generation to generation.
- **Technology.** Humans invent and mass-produce infinitely more complex and diverse artifacts than other animals.

The extraterrestrials might well be charmed by the elephant's trunk and impressed by the giraffe's neck, but it is humans that they would single out. –K.L.

Referenced

Social Intelligence, Innovation, and Enhanced Brain Size in Primates. Simon M. Reader and Kevin N. Laland in *Proceedings of the National Academy of Sciences USA*, Vol. 99, No. 7, pages 4436–4441; April 2, 2002.

Why Copy Others? Insights from the Social Learning Strategies Tournament. L. Rendell et al. in *Science*, Vol. 328, pages 208–213; April 9, 2010.

Identification of the Social and Cognitive Processes underlying Human Cumulative Culture. L. G. Dean et al. in *Science*, Vol. 335, pages 1114–1118; March 2, 2012.

About the Author

Kevin Laland is a professor of behavioral and evolutionary biology at the University of St. Andrews in Scotland and author of Darwin's Unfinished Symphony: How Culture Made the Human Mind *(Princeton University Press, 2017).*

Is "Junk DNA" What Makes Humans Unique?

By Zach Zorich

The things that separate chimpanzees from humans appear obvious on the surface. Humans are more graceful ice skaters, and we wear tuxedos with more panache than our closest primate relatives. We are, however, strikingly similar species on the level of our genes. The parts of our DNA that contain instructions for making proteins–the building blocks of our bodies–differ by less than 1 percent, but protein-coding genes are only a small part of our genomes. Some of the biggest differences between humans and chimps lie in the DNA that resides outside of genes.

About 10 years ago Katherine Pollard, a biostatistician at the Gladstone Institutes and the University of California, San Francisco, compared the two species and identified the parts of the human genome that are unique. Now she is leading a research team that is uncovering how 716 of these human-specific DNA regions work together to create the biological traits that differentiate us from other primates.

Most of these 700 some pieces of DNA lay outside of our genes, and Pollard's latest study partially solves the mystery of their function. By adapting new techniques from biotechnology, the U.C.S.F. scientists were able to engineer thousands of human and chimpanzee brain cells and test how these 716 "human accelerated regions" (HARs) affected the development of cells from both species. In the process her team has uncovered possible new targets for the treatment of autism, schizophrenia and other neuropsychiatric disorders. The study, which has not yet been peer-reviewed, was posted to the preprint server bioRxiv on January 30.

Since Pollard first published her research on HARs in 2006, deciphering their biological function has been slow going. At that time the only option for studying HARs was to painstakingly splice a single HAR into the DNA of a fertilized mouse egg and observe its effect on the mouse once the animal reached maturity. To make a comprehensive study of the way all of the HARs affect human biology, she needed a much faster way to study them.

A few years ago Pollard began working with Nadav Ahituv, a geneticist who runs a separate lab at U.C.S.F., to create a method for converting human and chimpanzee skin cells into pluripotent stem cells, which have the potential to become nearly any other cell type. The team could have chosen to coax them into liver, heart or bone cells, but for their first study of HARs the obvious choice was the cells that affect our species's most distinctive trait–intelligence. Pollard and Ahituv created thousands of neurons at a time and spliced the HAR DNA into those cells. Then they examined what the HARs did at two different points in the cells' development.

They found almost half of these pieces of DNA–which do not appear naturally in the chimpanzee genome–were active in the growing neurons. But the HARs were not producing proteins; they were in the part of the genome scientists once referred to as "junk DNA," and they were controlling the amount of proteins produced by the neurons' genes. The result surprised Ahituv: "This is the first comprehensive study of all these sequences, and it shows that 43 percent of them...could have a functional role in neural development."

According to Pollard, the parts of the chimpanzee genome that are analogous to the HARs have not changed at all in millions of years, and they are nearly identical to the same regions in most animals. Pollard says natural selection was acting to keep these parts of these animals' genomes from changing, but something must have happened to relieve that evolutionary pressure from humans after our ancestors split from chimps about 6 million years ago. "Most of [the HARs] have so many changes in them that not only did they acquire random mutations, but...the individuals carrying those changes produced more offspring," Pollard says. What happened to cause this is an open question. The fact that so many HARs are involved in neuronal development suggests the change may have had something to do with the evolution of intelligence, a vastly complicated trait that is the product of hundreds of mutations in our genomes.

These changes, however, came with some severe downsides. "A lot of these HARs lie near genes that are associated with human-specific disease like autism, schizophrenia and so forth," Ahituv says. This result suggests these diseases are not caused by brain-development genes themselves but by the way HARs regulate them. Part of Pollard and Ahituv's research focused on deciphering how each individual mutation within seven different HARs altered a gene's activity. The team found the individual mutations would increase or decrease the amount of protein a gene was producing. Essentially, natural selection was fine-tuning how the genes were expressed because too much or too little of a specific protein can cause problems. In autism, Pollard explains, "lots of mutations in different parts of the genome are coming together and all making small changes that together put an individual over a threshold where we would say they have autism." She adds: "The rest of us have some of those mutations and are just below that threshold."

The experimental approach Pollard and Ahituv used in this study may be able to show medical researchers what parts of the genome to target for new therapies. Maria Chahrour, an autism researcher at The University of Texas Southwestern Medical Center who was not part of the work, has been facing this problem as she tries to understand how autism manifests itself in the genome. "We are doing a lot of whole genome sequencing that will identify a lot of variants in noncoding regions of the genome," she says. "Now when we find disease variants in these HAR regions we are not going to dismiss them."

Pollard and Ahituv have received funding from the National Institutes of Health to study the contribution of HARs to brain evolution and their role in disease. They will also be examining how these bits of the genome are involved in the development of sperm and other types of cells. The ability to examine noncoding regions of genomes in thousands of cells at the same time could provide a powerful way to tackle a variety of questions about the genomes of humans as well as other organisms. It may also be the next-best thing to a time machine for learning about the genetic changes that led to the evolution of the modern human species. "We'll never see what happened in the past in evolutionary time," Pollard says, "but we were able re-create [this past] in the lab and measure its function."

About the Author

Zach Zorich is a freelance writer and a contributing editor at Archaeology Magazine.

What Makes Humans Different Than Any Other Species

By Gary Stix

At a psychology laboratory in Leipzig, Germany, two toddlers eye gummy bears that lie on a board beyond their reach. To get the treats, both tots must pull in tandem on either end of a rope. If only one child pulls, the rope detaches, and they wind up with nothing.

A few miles away, in a plexiglass enclosure at Pongoland, the ape facility at the Leipzig Zoo, researchers repeat the identical experiment, but this time with two chimpanzees. If the primates pass the rope-and-board test, each one gets a fruit treat.

By testing children and chimps in this way, investigators hope to solve a vexing puzzle: Why are humans so successful as a species? *Homo sapiens* and *Pan troglodytes* share almost 99 percent of their genetic material. Why, then, did humans come to populate virtually every corner of the planet–building the Eiffel Tower, Boeing 747s and H-bombs along the way? And why are chimps still foraging for their supper in the dense forests of equatorial Africa, just as their ancestors did 7 or so million years ago, when archaic humans and the great apes separated into different species?

As with any event that occurred on the time scale of evolution–hundreds of thousands or millions of years in the making–scientists may never reach a consensus on what really happened. For years the prevailing view was that only humans make and use tools and are capable of reasoning using numbers and other symbols. But that idea fell by the wayside as we learned more about what other primates are capable of. A chimp, with the right coach, can add numbers, operate a computer and light up a cigarette.

At present, the question of why human behavior differs from that of the great apes, and how much, is still a matter of debate. Yet experiments such as the one in Leipzig, under the auspices of the Max Planck Institute for Evolutionary Anthropology, have revealed a compelling possibility, identifying what may be a unique, but easy to overlook, facet of the human cognitive apparatus. From before their first birthday—a milestone some psychologists term "the nine-month revolution"—children begin to show an acute awareness of what goes on inside their mother's and father's heads. They evince this new ability by following their parents' gaze or looking where they point. Chimps can also figure out what is going on in a companion's mind to some degree, but humans take it one step further: infant and elder also have the ability to put their heads together to focus on what must be done to carry out a shared task. The simple act of adult and infant rolling a ball back and forth is enabled by this subtle cognitive advantage.

Some psychologists and anthropologists think that this melding of minds may have been a pivotal event that occurred hundreds of thousands of years ago and that shaped later human evolution. The ability of small bands of hunter-gatherers to work together in harmony ultimately set off a cascade of cognitive changes that led to the development of language and the spread of diverse human cultures across the globe.

This account of human psychological evolution, synthesized from bits and pieces of research on children and chimps, is speculative, and it has its doubters. But it provides perhaps the most impressively broad-ranging picture of the origins of cognitive abilities that make humans special.

The Ratchet Effect

The Max Planck Institute maintains the world's largest research facility devoted to examining the differences in behavior between humans and the great apes. Dozens of studies may be running at any one time. Researchers can draw subjects from a database of more than 20,000 children and recruit chimpanzees or members of any of the other great ape species—orangutans, bonobos and gorillas—from the Wolfgang Köhler Primate Research Center at the Leipzig Zoo a few miles away.

The institute began 17 years ago, seven years after the reunification of Germany. Founding the institute required coming to grips with the tarnished legacy of German anthropology–and its association with Nazi racial theories and, in particular, the grisly human experiments performed in Auschwitz by Josef Mengele, who was a physician with a doctorate in anthropology. The institute's organizers went out of their way to recruit group leaders for genetics, primatology, linguistics and other disciplines who were not native Germans.

One of them was Michael Tomasello, a tall, bearded psychologist and primatologist. Now 64, he grew up in a small citrus-growing city at the epicenter of the Florida peninsula. He began his academic career at the University of Georgia with a dissertation on the way toddlers acquire language. While he was doing his doctorate in the 1970s, linguists and psychologists often cited language as exhibit number one for human exceptionalism in the animal world.

Tomasello's doctoral thesis chronicled how his almost two-year-old daughter learned her first verbs. The emergence of proto words–"play play" or "ni ni"–revealed a natural inclination of the young child to engage in trial-and-error testing of language elements, an exercise that gradually took on the more conventional structuring of grammar and syntax. This learning process stood in contrast to the ideas of Noam Chomsky and other linguists who contended that grammar is somehow genetically hardwired in our brains–an explanation that struck Tomasello as reductionist. "Language is such a complicated thing that it couldn't have evolved like the opposable thumb," he says.

His work on language broadened his thinking about the relation between culture and human evolution. Tomasello realized that selective forces alone, acting on physical traits, could not explain the emergence of complex tools, language, mathematics and elaborate social institutions in the comparatively brief interval on the evolutionary timeline since humans and chimps parted ways. Some innate mental capacity displayed by hominins (modern humans and our extinct relatives) but absent in nonhuman primates must have enabled our forebears to behave in ways that vastly hastened the ability to feed and clothe themselves and to flourish in any environment, no matter how forbidding.

When Tomasello moved to a professorship at Emory University during the 1980s, he availed himself of the university's Yerkes primate research center to look for clues to this capacity in studies comparing the behaviors of children with those of chimps. The move set in motion a multidecade quest that he has continued at Max Planck since 1998.

In his studies of chimp learning, Tomasello noticed that apes do not ape each other the way humans imitate one another. One chimp might emulate another chimp using a stick to fetch ants out of a nest. Then others in the group might do the same. As Tomasello looked more closely, he surmised that chimps were able to understand that a stick could be used for "ant dipping," but they were unconcerned with mimicking one technique or another that might be used in hunting for the insects. More important, there was no attempt to go beyond the basics and then do some tinkering to make a new and improved ant catcher.

In human societies, in contrast, this type of innovation is a distinguishing characteristic that Tomasello calls a "ratchet effect." Humans modify their tools to make them better and then pass this knowledge along to their descendants, who make their own tweaks–and the improvements ratchet up. What starts as a lobbed stone projectile invented to kill a mammoth evolves over the millennia into a slingshot and then a catapult, a bullet, and finally an intercontinental ballistic missile.

This cultural ratchet provides a rough explanation for humans' success as a species but leads to another question: What specific mental processes were involved in transmitting such knowledge to others? The answer has to begin with speculations about changes in hominin physiology and behavior that may have taken place hundreds of thousands of years ago. One idea–the social brain hypothesis, put forward by anthropologist Robin Dunbar of the University of Oxford–holds that group size, and hence cultural complexity, scales up as brains get bigger. And scientists know that by 400,000 years ago, *Homo heidelbergensis*, probably our direct ancestor, had a brain almost as large as ours.

Tomasello postulates that, equipped with a bigger brain and confronted with the need to feed a growing population, early hominins began careful strategizing to track and outwit game. The circumstances exerted strong selection pressures for cooperation: any member of a hunting party who was not a team player–taking on a carefully defined role when tracking and cornering an animal–would have been excluded from future outings and so might face an unremittingly bleak future. If one hunter was a bad partner, Tomasello notes, the rest of the group would then decide: "We won't do this again." In his view, what separated modern humans from the hominin pack was an evolutionary adaptation for hypersociality.

The paleoarchaeological record of bones and artifacts is too scant to provide support for Tomasello's hypothesis. He draws his evidence from a comparison of child and chimp–matching our closest primate relative with a toddler who has yet to master a language or be exposed to formal schooling. The untutored child allows researchers to assess cognitive skills that have yet to be fully shaped by cultural influences and so can be considered to be innate.

Studies in Leipzig during the past decade or so have uncovered more similarities than differences between humans and chimps, but they also highlight what Tomasello calls "a small difference that made a big difference." One immense research undertaking, led by Esther Herrmann of the developmental and comparative psychology department at the Max Planck Institute under Tomasello's tutelage, ran from 2003 until its publication in Science in 2007. It entailed administering multiple cognitive tests to 106 chimpanzees at two African wildlife sanctuaries, 32 orangutans in Indonesia and 105 toddlers, aged two and a half years, in Leipzig.

The investigators set out to determine whether humans' bigger brain meant the children were smarter than great apes and, if so, what being smarter meant, exactly. The three species were tested on spatial reasoning (such as looking for a hidden reward), an ability to discriminate whether quantities were large or small, and an understanding of cause-and-effect relationships. It turned out that the toddlers and the chimpanzees scored almost identically on these tests (orangutans did not perform quite as well).

When it came to social skills, though, there was no contest. Toddlers bested both chimps and orangutans on tests (adapted for nonverbal apes) that examined the ability to communicate, learn from others, and evaluate another being's perceptions and wishes. The researchers interpreted the results as showing that human children are not born with a higher IQ (general reasoning capacities) but rather come equipped with a special set of abilities—"cultural intelligence," as the *Science* study put it—that prepares them for learning later from parents, teachers and playmates. "It was really the first time that it was shown that social-cognitive abilities are the key skills that make us special in comparison to other animals," Herrmann says.

Digging deeper required probing for the specific psychological processes that underlie humans' ultrasocial tendencies. Tomasello's research showed that at about nine months of age, parent and child engage in a figurative form of mind reading. Each has what psychologists call a "theory of mind." Each is aware of what the other one knows when they look together at a ball or block and play a little game with it. Each carries a mental image of these items in the same way a group of *H. heidelbergensis* would have all visualized a deer intended as dinner. This capacity to engage with another person to play a game or achieve a common goal is what Tomasello calls shared intentionality (a term he borrowed from philosophy). In Tomasello's view, shared intentionality is an evolutionary adaptation unique to humans—a minute difference with momentous consequences, rooted in an inherited predisposition for a degree of cooperative social interactions that is absent in chimps or any other species.

The Benefits of Mind Reading

The institute researchers noted that chimps, too, can read one another's minds to some degree. But their natural inclination is to use whatever they learn in that way to outcompete one another in the quest for food or mates. The chimp mind, it appears, is involved in a kind of Machiavellian mental scheming—"If I do this, will he do that?"—as Tomasello explains it. "It is inconceivable," he said in an October 2010 talk at the University of Virginia, "that you would ever see two chimpanzees carrying a log together."

The Leipzig researchers formally demonstrated the differences that separate the two species in the rope-and-board experiment, in which two chimpanzees at the Leipzig Zoo could get a snack of fruit only if they both pulled a rope attached to a board. If food was placed at both ends of the board, the apes took the fruit closest to them. If the treats were placed in the middle, however, the more dominant ape would grab the food, and after a few trials, the subordinate simply stopped playing. In the institute's child lab, the children worked together, whether the gummy bears were placed in the middle or at the ends of the board. When the treat was in the middle, the three-year-olds negotiated so that each would get an equal share.

Ancestral humans' mutual understanding of what was needed to get the job done laid the basis for the beginnings of social interactions and a culture based on cooperation, Tomasello argues. This "common ground," as he calls it, in which members of a group know much of what others know, may have opened the way for development of new forms of communication.

An ability to devise and perceive shared goals—and to intuit immediately what a hunting partner was thinking—apparently allowed our hominin ancestors to make cognitive strides in other ways, such as developing more sophistication in communicative uses of gesturing than our ape relatives possess.

The basic gestural repertoire of our hominin kin may have once been similar to that of the great apes. Archaic humans may have pointed, as chimpanzees do today, to convey commands—"Give me this" or "Do that"—a form of communication centered on an individual's needs. Chimps, perhaps reminiscent of humans in a primeval past, still make no attempt to use these gestures for teaching or passing along information.

For humans, gesturing took on new meaning as their mental-processing abilities got better. A hunter would point to a glade in the forest to indicate where a deer was grazing, an action immediately understood by a nearby companion. The way such pointing can take on new meanings is evident in modern life. "If I point to indicate 'Let's go have a cup of coffee over there,' it's not in the language," Tomasello says. "The meaning of 'that café' is in the finger, not in the language."

Young children understand this type of pointing, but chimps do not. This difference became evident in one study in which the experimenter repeatedly put blocks on a plate that the child needed for building a tower, which the child then used. At a certain juncture, there were no objects left when needed, and so the infant started pointing to the now empty plate, indicating that she wanted one of the blocks that were no longer there. The child knew that the adult would make the correct inference–the ability to refer to an absent entity is, in fact, a defining characteristic of human language. At the zoo, chimps put through a similar exercise–with food substituted for blocks–did not lift a finger when facing a vacant plate.

Only slightly older children start to understand gestures that pantomime an action–moving a hand to one's mouth to represent hunger or thirst. Chimps seeing these gestures during a study remain clueless. An ape will understand what is happening when a human applies a hammer to a nut to get the meat but is befuddled when that same person makes a pounding motion on the hand to convey the idea of carrying out the same action.

This type of gesturing–an extension of humans' cognitive capacity for shared intentionality–may have been the basis for communicating abstract ideas needed to establish more elaborate social groups, whether they be a tribe or a nation. Pantomiming would have enabled people to create story lines, such as conveying "the antelope grazes on the other side of the hill" by holding both hands in a V pattern on the top of one's head to signify the animal and then raising and lowering the hands to depict the hill. These scenarios derive from comparative experiments demonstrating that toddlers have an intuitive understanding of iconic gestures for many familiar activities but that chimpanzees do not.

Some of this gesturing occurred perhaps not just through moving the hands but also through vocalizations intended to represent specific objects or actions. These guttural noises may have evolved into speech, further enhancing the ability to manage complex social relationships as populations continued to grow–and rivalries arose among tribal groups. A group adept at working together would outcompete those that bickered among themselves.

Humans' expanding cognitive powers may have promoted specific practices for hunting, fishing, plant gathering or marriage that turned into cultural conventions–the way "we" do things–that the group as a whole was expected to adopt. A collection of social norms required each individual to gain awareness of the values shared by the group–a "group-mindedness" in which every member conformed to an expected role. Social norms produced a set of moral principles that eventually laid a foundation for an institutional framework–governments, armies, legal and religious systems–to enforce the rules by which people live. The millennial journey that began with a particular mind-set needed by bands of hunters now scaled up to entire societies.

Chimps and other great apes never got started down this path. When chimps hunt together to prey on colobus monkeys in Ivory Coast, this activity, as Tomasello interprets it, entails every chimp trying to run down the monkey first to get the most meat, whereas human hunter-gatherers, even in contemporary settings, cooperate closely as they track game and later share the spoils equitably. Tomasello concludes that ape societies and those of other foragers such as lions may appear to cooperate, but the dynamics at play within the group are still fundamentally competitive in nature.

The Great Debate

Tomasello's version of an evolutionary history is not universally accepted, even within the institution. One floor up from his office, in the department of primatology, Catherine Crockford talks me though a video her graduate student Liran Samuni made in March. It shows a young chimpanzee in the Taï National Park in Ivory Coast near the Liberian border.

The chimp the researchers call Shogun has just caught a large, black-and-white colobus monkey. Shogun is having trouble eating his still-alive and squirming catch and issues a series of sharp "recruitment screams" to summon help from two elder hunters lodged in the tree canopy. Kuba, one of the two, arrives on the scene shortly, and Shogun calms down a bit and takes his first real bite. But then Shogun continues to scream until the other hunter, Ibrahim, shows up. The younger ape puts his finger in Ibrahim's mouth as a "reassurance gesture," a mannerism that ensures that all is well. Ibrahim gives the sought-for emotional support by not biting Shogun's finger. The three then share the meal. "It's interesting that he's recruiting these two dominant males that could take this whole monkey from him," Crockford says. "But as you can see, they're not taking it from him. He's still allowed to eat it."

Crockford argues that it is still too early to draw conclusions about the extent to which chimps cooperate. "I don't think we know the limits of what chimps are doing," she says. "I think [Tomasello's] arguments are brilliant and really clear in terms of our current knowledge, but I think that with new tools that we're taking to the field, we'll find out whether the current limits are the limits of what chimps can do or not." Crockford is working with several other researchers to develop tests that would identify the social-bonding hormone oxytocin in chimpanzee urine. Some studies have shown that the hormone rises when chimps share food, a sign that the animals may cooperate when feeding.

Crockford did her doctoral studies at the institute in Leipzig, with both Tomasello and Christophe Boesch, head of the Max Planck Institute's department of primatology. Boesch has argued against Tomasello's conclusions by highlighting his own extensive research in the Taï National Park showing that chimps have a highly collaborative social structure–one chimp steers the monkey prey in the desired direction; others block its path along the way or take on yet additional roles. Boesch's views on chimp cooperation are similar to those of

Frans de Waal of the Yerkes National Primate Research Center at Emory. Still others criticize Tomasello from a diametrically opposing viewpoint. Daniel Povinelli of the University of Louisiana at Lafayette contends that Tomasello overstates chimps' cognitive capacities in suggesting that they have some ability to understand the psychological state of others in the group.

For his part, Tomasello seems to enjoy being in the midst of this academic jousting, saying: "In my mind, Boesch and de Waal are anthropomorphizing apes, and Povinelli is treating them like rats, and they're neither." He adds, jokingly, "We're in the middle. Since we're getting attacked equally from both sides, we must be right."

Condemnation from some quarters is tempered by a deep respect from others. "I used to think that humans were very similar to chimps," says Jonathan Haidt, a leading social scientist at the New York University Stern School of Business. "Over the years, thanks in large part to Tomasello's work, I've come to believe that the small difference he has studied and publicized–the uniquely human ability to do shared intentionality–took us over the river to a new shore, where social life is radically different."

Resolving these debates will require more research from zoo, lab and field station–perhaps through new studies on the extent to which chimps have a theory of mind about others. Still other research already under way by Tomasello's group is intended to determine whether the conclusions about human behavior, drawn from tests on German children, carry over if similar tests are performed on children in Africa or Asia. One study asks whether German preschoolers share their collective sense of what is right or wrong with the Samburu, a seminomadic people in northern Kenya.

There may also be room to look more deeply at human-ape differences. One of Tomasello's close longtime colleagues, Josep Call, who heads the Wolfgang Köhler Center, thinks that shared intentionality alone may not suffice to explain what makes humans special. Other cognitive capacities, he says, may also differentiate humans from other primates–one example may be "mental time travel"–our ability to imagine what may happen in the future.

More perspective on the overlap between humans and chimps may come from looking inside the human brain—an endeavor that is ongoing on yet another floor at Max Planck. Svante Pääbo, who led a team that finished an initial sequencing of the Neandertal genome in 2010, conjectures in a recent book that Tomasello's ideas about the uniqueness of human thinking may ultimately be tested through genetic analyses.

When those studies begin, a logical place to start would be to fuse research on chimp and human behaviors with the quixotic journey to understand the interactions among the hundreds of genes involved in autism. Children with the disorder, not unlike chimps, have difficulty understanding social cues. Comparing the genes in children with autism with those in unaffected children—and then with the DNA of chimps and perhaps even Neandertals, our closest evolutionary cousins—may yield a better understanding of a genetic basis for human sociality.

These investigations may also help explain why, over millennia, we progressed from bands of foragers to societies that not only provide food and shelter more efficiently than chimps do but also offer unceasing opportunities for social dealings—chances to move to any corner of the planet within a day's time or to convey messages to Tucson or Timbuktu as fast as a thought comes to mind.

Referenced

Cultural Origins of Human Cognition. Michael Tomasello. Harvard University Press, 1999.

Humans Have Evolved Specialized Skills of Social Cognition: The Cultural Intelligence Hypothesis. Esther Herrmann, Josep Call, María Victoria Hernàndez-Lloreda, Brian Hare and Michael Tomasello in *Science*, Vol. 317, pages 1360–1366; September 7, 2007.

A Natural History of Human Thinking. Michael Tomasello. Harvard University Press, 2014.

About the Author

Gary Stix is a senior editor at Scientific American.

Section 3: Invention and Innovation

Ancient Stone Tools Force Rethinking of Human Origins

By Kate Wong

The desert badlands on the northwestern shores of Kenya's Lake Turkana offer little to the people who live there. Drinking water is elusive, and most of the wild animals have declined to near oblivion. The Turkana scrape by as pastoralists, herding goats, sheep, cattle, donkeys and the occasional camel in the hot, arid countryside. It is a hard life. But millions of years ago the area brimmed with freshwater, plants and animals. It must have been paradise for the human ancestors who settled here.

Sonia Harmand has come to this region to study the legacy these ancestors left in stone. Harmand is an archaeologist at Stony Brook University. She has an intense gaze and a commanding presence. On a hazy July morning Harmand sits at a small, wood folding table, scrutinizing a piece of rock. It is brownish-gray, about the size of her pinkie fingernail, and utterly unremarkable to the untrained eye. But it is exactly what she has been looking for.

Nearby 15 workers from Kenya, France, the U.S. and England are digging their way into the side of a low hill. They tap hammers against chisels to chip away at the buff-colored sediments, searching for any bits of rock that could signal ancient human activity. At the top of the hill, the workers' water bottles hang like Christmas ornaments on the thorny branches of an acacia tree; the early breeze will keep their contents cool a little longer before the heat of the day sets in. By afternoon the air temperature will top 100 degrees Fahrenheit, and the excavation floor, windless and sun-cooked, will live up to its nickname: the Oven.

In 2015 Harmand and her husband, Jason Lewis, a paleoanthropologist at Stony Brook, announced that their team had discovered 3.3-million-year-old stone tools at this site, which is called Lomekwi 3. They were the oldest stone tools ever found by far—so old that they challenged a cherished theory of human evolution. The scientists want to learn who made the tools and why. But they also have a more immediate task: unearthing more evidence that the tools are, in fact, as old as they appear.

The fragment in Harmand's hand is the first evidence of ancient stone-tool production the researchers have recovered since they got here. It is a piece of debris produced by knapping—the act of striking one rock against another to produce a sharp-edged flake. Small and light, the fragment implies that the site has not been disturbed by flowing water in the millions of years since. That fact, in turn, supports the argument that the Lomekwi 3 tools come from this ancient sedimentary layer and not a younger one. Now that the excavators have hit the artifact-bearing level of the site, they must proceed with care. "*Pole pole*," Harmand instructs them in Swahili. Slowly, slowly.

Paleoanthropologists have long viewed stone-tool production as one of the defining characteristics of the *Homo* genus and the key to our evolutionary success. Other creatures use tools, but only humans shape hard materials such as rock to suit their purposes. Moreover, humans alone build on prior innovations, ratcheting up their utility—and complexity—over time. "We seem to be the only lineage that has gone fully technological," says Michael Haslam, an independent researcher. "It isn't even a crutch. It's like an addition to our bodies."

The conventional wisdom holds that our techno dependence began to form during a period of global climate change between 3 million and 2 million years ago, when Africa's woodlands transformed into savanna grasslands. Hominins, members of the human family, found themselves at a crossroads. Their old food sources were vanishing. They had to adapt or face extinction. One lineage, that of the so-called robust australopithecines, coped by evolving huge molars and powerful jaws to process the tougher plant foods available in grassland environments. Another—the larger-brained *Homo*—invented stone tools that gave it access to a wide variety of food sources, including the animals that grazed on these new plants. With the rich stores of calories from meat, *Homo* could afford to fuel an even bigger brain, which could then invent new and better tools for getting still more calories. In short order, a feedback loop formed, one that propelled our brain size and powers of innovation to ever greater heights. By 1 million years ago the robust australopithecines disappeared, and *Homo* was well on its way to conquering the planet.

The Lomekwi tools have smashed that scenario to pieces. Not only are they too old to belong to *Homo*, but they also predate the climate shift that supposedly kindled our ancestors' drive to create. And without any cut-marked bones or other signs of butchery at the site, it is not at all certain that the tools were used to process animal foods. What is more, such a vast expanse of time separates the Lomekwi tools from the next oldest implements on record that it is impossible to connect them to the rest of humanity's technological endeavoring, suggesting that the advent of stone tools was not necessarily the watershed moment that experts have always envisioned it to be.

These new discoveries have scientists scrambling to figure out when and how our predecessors acquired the cognitive and physical traits needed to conceptualize and fashion stone tools and to pass their craft to the next generation. If multiple lineages made tools from rock, researchers will need to rethink much of what they thought they knew about the origins of technology and how it shaped our branch of the family tree.

Dawn breaks gently in the bush—a slow brightening of sky, a creeping swell of birdsong—and the team's campsite, on the bank of a dry riverbed about a mile from Lomekwi 3, comes to life. By 6:30 A.M. the workers emerge from their tents and head to the makeshift dining table for breakfast, walking along a gravel path lined with stones to deter the snakes and scorpions. Within the hour they pile into Land Cruisers and set off on a bone-rattling ride to the excavation.

The team is down one vehicle and short on seats in the remaining two, so archaeologist Hélène Roche has decided to stay at camp.

Roche is an emeritus director of research at the French National Center for Scientific Research and an expert in early stone-tool technologies. She has short, sand-colored hair, and she dresses in desert hues. Her voice is low and crisp. Roche led the archaeological research in western Turkana for 17 years before handing the reins to Harmand and Lewis in 2011. She has returned for the second half of this expedition to see how they are faring. I remain at camp for the day to ask her about the history of work in this region.

"When I started in archaeology, we were just getting used to having stone tools at 1.8 [million years ago] at Olduvai," Roche recalls. In 1964 Kenyan paleoanthropologist Louis Leakey announced that he had found *Homo*-like fossils in association with what were then the oldest known artifacts in the world, stone tools from Tanzania's Olduvai Gorge (referred to as Oldowan tools). He assigned the fossils to a new species, *Homo habilis*, the "handy man," cementing the idea that stone toolmaking was linked to the emergence of *Homo*.

Hints that stone tools might have originated before *Homo* soon arrived, however. In the 1970s Roche, then a graduate student, discovered older Oldowan stone tools at a site in Ethiopia called Gona. When archaeologist Sileshi Semaw, now at the National Center for Research on Human Evolution in Burgos, Spain, and his colleagues eventually analyzed the tools, they reported them to be 2.6 million years old. Because no hominin remains turned up with the tools, researchers could not be sure which species made them. Semaw and his team proposed that a small-brained australopithecine species found at a different site nearby—*Australopithecus garhi*—was the toolmaker. Few were swayed by that argument, however. *Homo* was still the favorite candidate, even though, at the time, the oldest known *Homo* fossil was only 2.4 million years old. (A recent find has extended the fossil record of Homo back to 2.8 million years ago.)

Yet as old as they were, the Gona artifacts looked too skillfully wrought to represent humanity's first foray into stone-tool manufacturing. So did other ancient tools that began to emerge, including some from western Turkana. In the 1990s Roche found 2.3-million-year-old Oldowan stone tools at a site five miles from here known as Lokalalei 2c. She realized that in many instances, the site preserved entire knapping sequences that she could piece together like a 3-D puzzle. By refitting the Lokalalei flakes to the cores from which they were detached, Roche and her colleagues could show that toolmakers struck as many as 70 flakes from a single core. This impressive feat required an understanding of the rock shape best suited to flaking (flat on one side and convex on the other) and careful planning to maintain that shape while knapping. "You cannot imagine what it is like to hold the pieces together and reconstruct what [the toolmaker] has done and how he has done it, to go inside the prehistoric mind," she says.

It was becoming clear that the sophistication evident in the tools from Gona, Lokalalei and elsewhere could not have sprung fully formed from the minds of these knappers. Some kind of technological tradition must have preceded the Oldowan.

In 2010 far older signs of stone-tool technology came to light. Zeresenay Alemseged, now at the University of Chicago, and his colleagues reported that they had found two animal bones bearing what appeared to be cut marks from stone tools at the site of Dikika in Ethiopia. The bones dated to 3.4 million years ago, hundreds of thousands of years before the earliest known traces of *Homo*. The researchers credited the marks to *Australopithecus afarensis*, a species that was still apelike in many respects, with about as much gray matter as a chimpanzee has and a body that retained some adaptations to life in the trees—hardly the brainy, fully terrestrial hominin that researchers had traditionally expected the first butcher to be. The claims did not go unchallenged, however. Some experts countered that animals could have trampled the bones. Without the stone tools themselves, the critics argued, the Dikika scars could not qualify as tool-inflicted marks—and the question of just how far back in time technology originated remained unresolved.

Around the time the battle over the Dikika bones erupted, Harmand and Lewis began to hatch a plan to look for the older stone tools that the Dikika marks, along with the too-good-to-be-first tools from Gona and Lokalalei, implied should exist. In the summer of 2011 they set out in search of new archaeological sites on the western side of Lake Turkana.

The Turkana basin, as well as much of the Great Rift Valley in which it sits, is a paleoanthropologist's dream. Not only does it harbor an abundance of fossils and artifacts, but it preserves them in rocks that, with some sleuthing, can be dated with a relatively high degree of certainty. The region's history of volcanic eruptions and fluctuating water levels is recorded in the layers of sediment that have accumulated over eons to form a sort of layer cake. Water and wind erosion have exposed cross sections of the cake in locations throughout the basin. Tectonic activity has pushed some sections higher and other sections lower than they once were, but as long as any given exposure preserves at least a few layers of the cake, researchers can figure out where in the geologic sequence it comes from and thus how old it is.

To navigate the rough, roadless landscape, the team drives in the dry riverbeds, called *lagas*, that snake through the region, running from the lake to points west. On July 9 of that year the researchers were headed to a site where, 12 years earlier, a different team had found a 3.5-million-year-old skull of another hominin species, *Kenyanthropus platyops*, when they took the wrong branch of the Lomekwi *laga* and got lost. Climbing a nearby hillside to get a better view of the terrain, they realized that they had ended up in just the kind of place that is promising for finding ancient remains. Outcrops of soft lake sediments, which tend to preserve fossils and artifacts well, surrounded them. And the researchers knew from previous geologic mapping of the region that all the sediments along this *laga* were more than 2.7 million years old. They decided to look around.

Within a couple of hours Sammy Lokorodi, one of the Turkana members of the team, found several rocks bearing hallmarks of knapping—adjacent, scoop-shaped scars where sharp flakes had been chipped off. Could these be the older, more primitive tools that the team was looking for? Maybe. But the tools were found on the surface. A modern-day human—perhaps a passing Turkana nomad–could have made them and left them there. The researchers knew that to make a convincing case that the tools were ancient, they would have to find more of them, sealed in sediments that had lain undisturbed since their deposition, and conduct detailed geologic analyses of the site to establish the age of the artifacts more precisely. Their work had just begun.

By the time the researchers went public with their discovery, describing it in 2015 in *Nature*, they had excavated 19 stone tools from a 140-square-foot area. And they had correlated the position of the sediment layer that held the tools to layers of rock with known ages, including a 3.31-million-year-old layer of compacted volcanic ash called the Toroto Tuff and a magnetically reversed layer from a time, 3.33 million years ago, when the earth's magnetic poles switched places. They had also located the source of the raw material for the tools–a 3.33-million-year-old layer of beach containing cobbles of volcanic basalt and phonolite, along with fish and crocodile fossils that show just how much higher lake levels were back then as compared with today. Together these clues indicated that the tools dated to a stunning 3.3 million years ago–700,000 years older than the Gona tools and half a million years older than the earliest fossil of *Homo*.

The artifacts have little in common with Oldowan tools. They are far larger, with some flakes the size of a human hand. And experiments indicate that they were knapped using different techniques. Oldowan knappers favored a freehand style, striking a hammerstone held in one hand against a core held in the other, Harmand explains. The Lomekwi knappers, in contrast, would either bang a core they held in both hands against an anvil lying on the ground or place a core on the anvil and hit it with a hammerstone. The methods and finished products demonstrate an understanding of the fracture mechanics of stone but show considerably less dexterity and planning than are evident in tools from Gona and Lokalalei. The researchers had found their pre-Oldowan stone-tool tradition. They call it the Lomekwian.

Not everyone is convinced that the Lomekwi tools are as old as the discovery team claims. Some skeptics contend that the team has not proved that the artifacts originated from the sediments dated to 3.3 million years ago. Discoveries made this field season, including the knapping debris, as well as a handful of new tools recovered during excavation, may help allay those concerns. But even researchers who accept the age and the argument that the rocks were shaped by hominins are grappling with what the find means.

First, who made the tools? To date, the team has not recovered any hominin remains from the site, apart from a single, enigmatic tooth. The age and geographical location of the tools suggest three possibilities: *K. platyops*, the only hominin species known to have inhabited western Turkana at the time; *A. afarensis*, the species found in association with the cut-marked animal bones from Dikika; and *Australopithecus deyiremeda*, a species that was recently named, based on a partial jawbone found in Ethiopia. Either *K. platyops* or *A. afarensis* would be surprising because both those species had a brain about the size of a chimp's—not the enlarged brain researchers thought the first toolmaker would have. (*A. deyiremeda*'s brain size is unknown.)

Small brain size is not the only anatomical trait that experts did not expect to see in an ancient knapper. Paleoanthropologists thought that tool use arose after our ancestors had abandoned life in the trees to become committed terrestrial bipeds. In this scenario, only after their hands had been freed from the demands of climbing could hominins evolve the hand shape needed to make stone tools. Yet studies of *A. afarensis*, the only one of these three species for which bones below the head have been found, indicate that although it was a capable biped on the ground, it retained some traits that would have allowed it to climb trees for food or safety. Just how important was the shift away from life in the trees to life on the ground in the emergence of stone-tool technology?

The Lomekwi 3 tools are also forcing scientists to reconsider why hominins invented stone tools to begin with. Reconstruction of the paleoenvironment of the greater Lomekwi area 3.3 million years ago indicates that it was wooded, not the savanna experts thought had forged *Homo*'s stone-working skills.

Perhaps the biggest question: Why are the Lomekwi 3 tools so isolated in time? If stone-tool manufacture was the game-changing development that experts have always thought it to be, why did it not catch on as soon as it first appeared and initiate the feedback loop that expanded the brain?

Recent studies may help explain how a hominin more primitive than *Homo* could have come to make stone tools. It turns out that some of the differences in cognitive ability between hominins and other primates may not be as great as previously thought.

Observations of our closest primate cousins, for example, hint that even though they do not manufacture stone tools in the wild, they possess many of the cognitive abilities needed to do so. David Braun of George Washington University and Susana Carvalho of the University of Oxford have found that in Bossou, Guinea, wild chimps that use stones to crack open nuts understand the physical properties of different rocks. The researchers shipped assorted stones from Kenya to Bossou and made them available to the chimps for their nut-cracking activities. Despite not having prior experience with these kinds of rock, the chimps consistently selected the ones with the best qualities for the job. And experiments with captive bonobos carried out by Nicholas Toth of the Stone Age Institute in Bloomington, Ind., and his colleagues have shown that they can be trained to make sharp flakes and use them to cut rope. "I have no doubt that our apes could replicate what [Harmand and her team] have at Lomekwi, given the right raw material," Toth asserts.

Even inventing stone tools in the first place may not have required special genius. In November 2016 Tomos Proffitt, now at University College London, and his colleagues reported that they had observed wild capuchin monkeys in Brazil's Serra da Capivara National Park unintentionally making sharp stone flakes that look for all the world like Oldowan tools. Quartzite cobbles abound in the monkeys' environment, and they will often pick up one cobble and bash it against another embedded in the ground that serves as an anvil. All the bashing dislodges sharp flakes that have the hallmarks of intentionally produced stone tools, including the scooplike shape that arises from what is known as conchoidal fracturing. The monkeys ignore the flakes, however. Instead they seem to be pulverizing the quartz to eat it–they pause between strikes to lick the resulting dust from the anvil. Perhaps early hominins invented their stone flakes by accident, too, or found naturally sharp stones in their environment, and only later, once they found a good use for them, began fashioning them on purpose.

The possibility that the Lomekwi toolmakers had hands that were at once capable of knapping and climbing in trees does not seem so improbable either, once one considers what our primate cousins can manage. The modern human hand, with its short, straight fingers and long, opposable thumb, is purpose-built for power, precision and dexterity–traits we exploit every time we swing a hammer, turn a key or send a text. Yet as the observations of chimps, bonobos and capuchins show, other primates with hands built for grasping tree branches can be surprisingly dexterous. The hands of partially arboreal hominins could have been similarly clever.

In fact, recent studies of the fossilized hand bones of three small-brained hominin species from South Africa–*Australopithecus africanus*, *Australopithecus sediba* and *Homo naledi*–show evidence for exactly this combination of activities. All three species have curved fingers–a trait associated with climbing. Yet in other respects, their hands look like those of toolmakers. Tracy Kivell and Matt Skinner, both at the University of Kent in England, examined the internal structure of the hand bones, which reflects the loading forces sustained in life, and found a pattern consistent with that seen in hominins known to have made and used stone tools and different from the internal structure of the hand bones of chimps. "Being a good climber and a dexterous toolmaker are not mutually exclusive," Kivell says. A variety of hand shapes can make and use stone tools, she explains. The changes the human hand eventually underwent just optimized it for the job.

Friday is choma night for the Lomekwi team–roasted goat will be served for dinner. Nick Taylor of Stony Brook, a droll Brit, is taking advantage of the menu to try to figure out what purpose the Lomekwi stone tools served. This morning one of the local Turkana shepherds brought the purchased animal for slaughter. This afternoon, as the sun begins its descent and meal preparations begin, Taylor asks camp kitchen manager Alfred "Kole" Koki to try to process the carcass with replicas of the Lomekwi tools. Koki, an experienced butcher, doubts they will work. But he gamely takes a two-inch-long flake and starts slicing. He manages to skin most of the animal and carves some of the meat with the sharp-edged rocks, discarding them as they become dull, before reclaiming his steel knife to finish the job.

Taylor observes how Koki instinctively holds each flake and how long it retains its edge before Koki requests a new one. Taylor keeps the used replica flakes so that later he and his colleagues can compare their damaged edges with those of the real flakes. He will also collect some of the bones to study what kind of cut marks the carving might have left on them. And he will try using the tools to cut plant materials, including wood and tubers. In addition, Taylor is looking for any residues on the Lomekwi tools that might provide clues to what they were processing.

For whatever reason the Lomekwi hominins made stone tools, their tradition does not appear to have stuck. Nearly 700,000 years separates their implements from the next oldest tools at Gona and a more recently discovered site in Ethiopia called Ledi-Geraru. Perhaps hominins did indeed have a stone-tool culture spanning that time, and archaeologists have just not found it yet. But maybe the Lomekwi stone-working was just a flash in the pan, unrelated to the Oldowan technology that followed. Even the Oldowan record is patchy and variable, showing different tool styles at different times and places, without much continuity among them. As Roche puts it, "There is not one Oldowan but Oldowans."

This pattern suggests to many archaeologists that populations in multiple lineages of hominins and possibly other primates may have experimented with stone-tool production independently, only to have their inventions fizzle out, unbequeathed to the next generation. "We used to think that once you have toolmaking, we're off to the races," observes Dietrich Stout of Emory University. But maybe with these early populations, he says, technology was not important to their adaptation, so it simply faded away.

Around 2 million years ago, however, something changed. The tools from this period start to look as though they were manufactured according to the same rules. By around 1.7 million years ago a more sophisticated technology arises: the Acheulean. Known for its hand ax, the Swiss Army knife of the Paleolithic, the Acheulean tradition spread across Africa and into other parts of the Old World.

Braun thinks the shift has to do with improved information transmission. Chimps appear to have what he calls low-fidelity transmission of behavior based on observational learning. It works pretty well for simple tasks: by the end of his team's six-week-long experiment with the Bossou chimps, the entire community was using the rocks the same way. The activity seemed to spread by means of a recycling behavior in which one individual, typically a juvenile, would watch another, usually an adult, use a certain type of rock to crack nuts, after which the youngster would try to use the adult's tool set to achieve the same ends.

Modern humans, in contrast, actively teach others how to do complex things–from baking a cake to flying a plane–which is a high-fidelity form of transmission. Perhaps, Braun suggests, the variability seen in the Lomekwi tools and in those of the early Oldowan is the result of lower-fidelity transmission, and the standardization of the later Oldowan and the more sophisticated Acheulean signals the development of a more effective means of sharing knowledge, one that allowed humans to ratchet up their technological complexity.

As ancient as the tools from Lomekwi 3 are, the team suspects that even older ones are out there, awaiting discovery. One day, while the rest of the team is excavating, Lewis, Lokorodi and Xavier Boës, a geologist at the French National Institute for Preventive Archaeological Research, set out to look for them. They head for an area known to have sediments older than those at Lomekwi 3, speeding up the *laga* in a cloud of dust. They are taking the same branch they meant to take on that day in 2011 when they lost their way and discovered Lomekwi 3.

When they reach their destination, they fan out, eyes trained on the ground, scanning for signs of human handiwork in a sea of rocks baked red by the sun. Before long, Lokorodi spies cobbles bearing scoop-shaped scars. In theory, they could be more than 3.5 million years old. But to make a compelling case, the researchers will have to determine whether the rocks have been shaped by humans and, if so, figure out which stratigraphic level they eroded from, pinpoint the age of that level and then find more of them undisturbed in the ground. Lewis photographs the rocks and notes their location for possible survey in the future. The team will also explore a promising area about three miles from Lomekwi 3 that has sediments dating to more than four million years ago.

Figuring out what technology came before and after Lomekwi 3 and getting a clearer picture of how the environment was shifting will be critical to elucidating the correlations among dietary change, tools and the origins of *Homo*. "Maybe the links are all the same, but everything happened earlier," Lewis offers. "The pieces have exploded, but that doesn't mean they won't reassemble."

"We know quite a lot now but not enough," Roche says of the discoveries in western Turkana. "This is only the beginning."

Referenced

3.3-Million-Year-Old Stone Tools from Lomekwi 3, West Turkana, Kenya. Sonia Harmand et al. in *Nature*, Vol. 521, pages 310–315; May 21, 2015.

Wild Monkeys Flake Stone Tools. Tomos Proffitt et al. in *Nature*, Vol. 539, pages 85–88; November 3, 2016.

About the Author

Kate Wong is a senior editor for evolution and ecology at Scientific American.

The Other Tool Users

By Michael Haslam

The tide is rising fast, but the monkeys don't seem to mind. They bicker and loll on the rocks and mangroves farther up the shore, munching quietly on an oyster or enjoying a gentle grooming. The younger ones make a game of jumping from a tree branch into the warm, clear sea below. Like everyone along this coastal stretch of rural Thailand, they live in tune with the daily tidal rhythms.

I, however, am quite concerned about the incoming water. It's a balmy December day in 2013, and I'm crouched on the beach beside a neat square hole, reaching as far down as I can to scrape out another trowel-full of damp sand. The hole is only half a meter on each side, but it has taken hours to dig, ever since the overnight high tide receded. Careless movement will collapse the entire thing in on itself, which means that rushing is not an option.

This is an archaeological dig, and it looks much like you might imagine, with buckets, sieves, strings, levels, collecting bags and measuring tapes strewn about. Yet the ancient objects that drew me here to the small island of Piak Nam Yai in Laem Son National Park are not typical archaeological finds. I am not looking for coins, or pottery, or the remains of an old settlement, or long-lost human culture. Instead I am after bygone traces of the monkey culture that is on full display up the beach.

I am, at least itinerantly, a primate archaeologist: I use traditional archaeological methods to understand the past behavior of a variety of primate species. To be honest, the image that I get when I use this phrase is of Dr. Cornelius, the chimpanzee in the original 1968 film *Planet of the Apes* who controversially unearths evidence that humans were not always mute beasts. He is charged with heresy for his discovery, and although it is not discussed in the film, I strongly suspect that he also loses his funding. Cornelius resonates with me because my colleagues and I have recently been building a new scientific field that directly mirrors his work. For more than 150 years the term "archaeology" has described the scientific study of physical remains of a strictly human past. In that time, there have emerged a multitude of subfields focused on specific times, places or methods, but they have all had one central theme: understanding people. Nonhuman animals were a part of archaeological study but only as food, transport, pets or parasites. They orbited our world.

Certainly this focus has produced extraordinary achievements. For instance, in 2015 Sonia Harmand of Stony Brook University and her team stretched the known record of human behavior back to more than 3 million years ago when they found stone tools left by a distant ancestor at the site of Lomekwi in Kenya. (The fact that these objects are made of stone is not a coincidence, by the way. For the vast majority of that multimillion-year record, stone tools have been the only cultural artifacts that have survived to guide our interpretations of our origins–objects made from more perishable materials have been lost to time.)

By turning the spotlight on our closest evolutionary relatives–monkeys and apes–primate archaeology aims to build a richer framework for understanding this long history of human technological development. Humans and our direct ancestors are primates, too, of course, and illuminating our own evolutionary journey is still a central goal of this research. Placing the surprisingly complex rise of human technology into its wider biological context will give us a better grip on those features that derive from our shared primate heritage and those that are truly unique to us.

Absence of Evidence

A big part of why archaeologists have traditionally focused exclusively on the recovery of human material culture is that for a long time, researchers thought that humans alone use and produce tools. Primatologist Jane Goodall was the first to show otherwise through her studies of chimpanzees in the 1960s. Anthropologist Louis Leakey had been discovering a variety of fossil humans and stone tools in ancient lakeshore environments in eastern Africa, and he wanted to know what kinds of activities the human ancestors there might have engaged in. So Leakey recruited Goodall and sent her to what is now Gombe Stream National Park, on the eastern shore of Lake Tanganyika in Tanzania, to see how the chimpanzees there behaved. Although her eventual discoveries had little to do with the actual lake, her observations of chimpanzees making and using tools to obtain food forever changed our perception of primate abilities. But the Gombe chimps (*Pan troglodytes schweinfurthii*) use tools only made from plants, which last a matter of weeks in the tropical climate. The mismatch in survival between the million-year-old stone tools found in abundance by Leakey and the sticks and grass tools found by Goodall was stark.

Fortunately, chimpanzees are an inventive lot, and in the 1970s researchers discovered several groups of the western subspecies (*Pan troglodytes verus*) using stone tools to crack open forest nuts. Genetic evidence suggests that this subspecies split from the main, central chimpanzee population perhaps half a million years ago. Given the lack of stone tool use among central or eastern chimpanzees (as seen at Gombe)—or among their sister species, bonobos (*Pan paniscus*)—it seems likely that the western population independently invented stone use since that time.

That discovery raised key questions about the origins of stone tools. Our common ancestor probably used plant tools, just as wild chimpanzees and bonobos, as well as orangutans and gorillas, do. But why did only a very few branches of the family tree look to stone as a raw material? Furthermore, wild chimps have a very limited range of uses for stones, based chiefly on the mechanical advantage gained by employing a hard rock to crack open a stubborn nutshell. Humans, on the other hand, used stones to develop everything from cutting tools to projectile tips, from jewelry to the pyramids of Egypt and Central America. Why do the technological trajectories of chimps and humans look so different?

With just two examples of stone tool technology, developed independently by humans and chimpanzees, the steps leading to its emergence are difficult to resolve. We cannot simply take what one subset of chimps do and map it onto our early ancestors, arguing that human technology arose from stone-tool-mediated nut cracking. It would make just as little sense to take what a subset of modern humans do and map it onto chimpanzee ancestors.

One of the main issues is that we have virtually no record of the evolution of chimpanzees. Mounting DNA evidence indicates that humans and chimps diverged from their common ancestor around 7 million years ago. Yet the only known chimpanzee fossils are three teeth dating to around half a million years ago. And the oldest known chimpanzee tools are little more than 4,000 years old. As a result, knowledge of our ape siblings is stuck in something of an eternal present, with our view of them almost entirely derived from the past few decades. If we evaluated humans over the same short time frame, we would gain very sparse understanding of how our technologies emerged and changed throughout our evolution. If we had to guess, would we consider chopsticks or cutlery to best represent ancestral human eating tools? Is the PlayStation or Xbox the more primitive form of a human plaything? These questions may seem slightly absurd, yet scientists often fail to consider whether past chimps behaved anything like those we see now. Were they less technologically proficient? Or more so?

Another central concern is that a two-way comparison offers few clues as to why certain features developed in one lineage and not the other. For example, as early as the 1860s, English naturalist John Lubbock (who coined the terms "Paleolithic" and "Neolithic" for chapters of the Stone Age) suggested that primate nut cracking could be a simple precursor of the human tendency to break stones against each other to create sharp-edged flakes for cutting. If so, why do living chimpanzees not flake stones? Does the absence of this behavior stem from a lack of imagination, time or opportunity? Ideally we would have a much broader selection of case studies to test our hypotheses about the development of technology. This is where the monkeys I have been studying clamber to our rescue.

Game of Stones

Back on the beach in Thailand, the bottom of the hole is now filling with water. It seeps in from the sides, threatening to undercut and destabilize the walls even further. I have rigged a boat pump to a car battery to keep the level down, but I am losing the battle. Finally, with the waves lapping at my toes, I carefully bring up a series of small volcanic rocks, each one bearing distinct scars and pits on their rough surface.

Thanks to work over the past decade by primatologists Suchinda Malaivijitnond of Chulalongkorn University in Thailand and Michael Gumert of Nanyang Technological University in Singapore, we now know that wild Burmese long-tailed macaques (*Macaca fascicularis aurea*) on Piak Nam Yai and other islands along the coast of the Andaman Sea regularly use stone tools. The behavior extends north from Thailand into Myanmar, where it was first described in the 1880s by Alfred Carpenter, a British sea captain. That report seems to have gone largely unnoticed, though, and it was only in early 2005, during surveys to assess the effects of the devastating Indian Ocean tsunami of 2004, that macaque tool use was rediscovered.

The macaques' use of stones seems to be entrenched, given the similarity of observations from the 19th and 21st centuries. Once the tide goes out, the monkeys come down from the interior forests of their island. They select roughly hand-sized stones from those lying on the shore and use them to strike and remove the upper shell of oysters attached to the now exposed rocks. They typically need only five or six strikes to open each oyster, and they carry around the same tool to use over and over again. In extreme cases, my team has seen them use one stone hammer to crack and consume more than 60 oysters in a row.

Oysters are not the only food for which the macaques need a utensil. Intertidal zones such as this one are rich with animal life. Although the macaques prefer oysters, they are also on the lookout for marine snails and crabs. Unlike oysters, these prey can and do run away, so the monkeys gather them up and take them to a nearby flat rock. They then find a much larger stone than the ones used for oyster pounding–the largest weigh several kilograms–and use it to crush their food against the flat rock, which serves as an anvil. When the group is midfeast, the constant cracking and rapping sounds of stone on shell fill the air.

The end result of these low-tide grab-and-smash raids is a shoreline strewn with broken shells and battered stones. The monkeys select their tools with skill and persistence, using the pointed ends of small rocks to precisely hit the oysters and the large central areas of the bigger rocks to pound open snails. These two main patterns of behavior damage the tools in predictable ways, and my colleagues and I have shown that how a macaque tool was used (and therefore its potential target prey) can be determined from wear, which is readily distinguished from scars seen on naturally modified stones. It is this characteristic damage that I search for as I dig into the soft beach sands. The small volcanic rocks that I have rescued from the tides bear the oyster-processing marks. Although these artifacts do not push back the known antiquity of macaque tool use–the oldest ones date to just 65 years ago–they are the first monkey tools ever found through archaeological excavation.

Capuchins and Cashews

These macaques are not the only monkeys that have left behind an archaeological record. Fast-forward to late 2014, and I am back beside a square hole, but this time there is no sea breeze to alleviate the heat. Surrounding me are the scrub forests and towering sandstone plateaus of the semiarid Serra da Capivara National Park in northeastern Brazil. A team of undergraduate students from a university in nearby São Raimundo Nonato is digging, while Tiago Falótico and Lydia Luncz–my primatologist postdoctoral researchers at the time–record the finds. Thankfully, there is no encroaching tide, just the occasional scorpion or spider objecting to us moving its leaf litter around.

We are here because the wild bearded capuchins (*Sapajus libidinosus*) that live in the park have proved themselves to be master technologists. In 2004 capuchin experts Dorothy Fragaszy of the University of Georgia and Elisabetta Visalberghi of the Institute of Cognitive Sciences and Technologies in Italy reported that they had observed wild capuchins in a similar habitat some 200 miles away using stone tools. Now we know that capuchins at a wide range of sites in Brazil's interior select and use heavy stones to break open the tough shells of the local nuts and fruits in a manner that superficially resembles the behavior of western chimpanzees. The capuchins in Serra da Capivara National Park are especially creative with their tools, however. In addition to cracking open nuts and fruits, they also use rocks to penetrate the soil and dig down in search of burrowing spiders and plant roots. In another parallel with their ape cousins, these capuchins also select and break off twigs and then bite them to size and strip the leaves to make probes that they use to hunt hard-to-reach prey, such as lizards hidden in crevices.

One food in particular has our eye during the excavation. Cashew trees are indigenous to this area of Brazil, although they are now grown commercially worldwide. Their nut is nutritious and tasty, but fresh cashews have a caustic liquid in their shell that painfully burns the skin. So the capuchins use heavy stone hammers to break into the nuts. Their tactic is effective and, lucky for us, leaves telltale impact marks and dark cashew liquid all over the tools. By surveying and mapping capuchin stones that have accumulated over several years of use, we were able to find the pockets of the forest most intensively exploited by the monkeys. Because the soil, moisture and shade conditions that suit cashew tree growth have not changed significantly over the past few thousand years, we reasoned that the sites that are heavily trafficked today probably also saw a lot of capuchin activity in the past. Our excavations at a selection of these sites bore this notion out. We found at least four distinct phases of former monkey tool use, reflected in groups of buried stone hammers and anvils with clear damage from use. Bolstering our conclusion that these were capuchin tools, we found no signs of human activity, whether fire or pottery, or any of the kinds of stone tools people are known to make.

The oldest layer with capuchin tools dates back to between 2,400 and 3,000 years ago. These implements are therefore the oldest known nonhuman artifacts outside Africa, and they record the behavior of monkeys living well before the European invasion of the Americas. We did not find any evidence of ancient plant tool use from our excavations, but as is true for humans and other apes, this absence probably reflects the usual bias toward the survival of rocks over sticks.

Finding tools of another monkey species through archaeological excavation would have been reward enough for our efforts. But the Serra da Capivara National Park capuchins had a surprise in store for us. During the same field season, I filmed the monkeys breaking hammer stones against other rocks that were embedded into a large conglomerate block. They seemed to be aiming to create quartz dust, which they then licked or sniffed. Other researchers had observed this behavior before, but when I collected the broken pieces of rock and later excavated around the conglomerate block, I noticed something that had not been reported previously: the capuchins' rock shards bore an unmistakable resemblance to the stone flakes seen at some early human ancestor sites. Detailed analysis of the stones by another of my then postdocs at the University of Oxford, Tomos Proffitt, proved that we had found the first example of a nonhuman primate deliberately breaking stones and leaving behind sharp-edged flakes.

To be clear, the capuchins have not yet been observed using the sharp flakes that they create. In the wild, that behavior remains exclusively human, for now. But if repeated flaking of stone hammers can be an unintended by-product of an until now unimagined activity—creating dust for ingestion—then this finding raises substantial questions about parts of the early human archaeological record. Archaeologists have tended to assume that early humans deliberately smashed rocks to create sharp flakes for a specific purpose—cutting meat, for example. Given what we see in the capuchins, however, we must ask ourselves whether our ancestors 3 million years ago might have been similarly uninterested in those sharp rocks they were making. Did they, too, produce accidental flakes for a considerable time before latching onto the idea of picking them up and cutting things? Honestly, we do not know. But now we must at least consider the possibility. It would certainly smooth the pathway for the uptake of cutting as an innovation if there was already a known and reliable way to make the tools, with sharp edges moving conceptually from hazardous waste to valuable resource.

Beyond Primates

Whatever the lessons for our own technological evolution, the finds from Brazil and Thailand mean that we now have archaeological records for three nonhuman primate lineages. It is worth pausing for a second to consider that fact. A mere decade ago we were learning of the existence of stone-tool-wielding wild monkeys. Now we have taken the first steps to trace that behavior back into deep time. The human line today forms only a quarter of the known primate archaeological records, albeit the best investigated portion by far.

In a recent paper, my colleagues and I suggested that we have reached the end of anthropocentric archaeology; going forward, archaeology has all past behavior in its sights. Some scholars may disagree with my contention that archaeology is just a method, applicable to any animal that leaves an enduring material record of its behavior, rather than something reserved for our own lineage. But the work of a small group of primate archaeologists has shown that it can open up new ways of viewing both our own evolutionary pathway and that of other species. Clearly, technology–the skilled and learned integration of material culture into our lives–is not a human-specific oddity. To evolve, it does not require language, or human-style teaching and cooperation, or even a large brain: the capuchins and macaques each have adult brains around 5 percent of the size of an adult human brain.

Moreover, stone tool use has emerged independently at least four times in relatively recent primate evolution: in coastal (macaque), lakeside (human), forested (chimpanzee) and semiarid (capuchin) environments. This diversity means we can reasonably expect that the same behavior has emerged repeatedly in the past, among many primate taxa, even if they no longer exhibit it or have gone extinct. Excitingly, if this scenario is true, the stone tools used by those taxa are still out there, waiting to be discovered.

There is no reason that we should stop at primates. In the past few years I have begun archaeological work with stone-tool-using wild sea otters on the West Coast of the U.S. in conjunction with ethologist Natalie Uomini of the Max Planck Institute for the Science of Human History in Jena, Germany, and other colleagues based at the Monterey Bay Aquarium and the University of California, Santa Cruz. We have learned, for instance, that the sea otters repeatedly return to favored places along the shoreline to break open shellfish, leaving behind damaged stones and large piles of discarded shells that could easily be mistaken for prehistoric human shell middens, or rubbish heaps. The feedback cycle between these durable landscape markers and their attraction for young animals learning to use tools may be a critical component of technological traditions among sea otters, much like the cycle between the prize cashew trees and the bearded capuchins.

Uomini and I have also conducted fieldwork on the archaeology of New Caledonian crows, which are famous for their sophisticated tool use and cognitive skills. New Caledonian crows regularly exploit specific locations on the landscape; once durable tool materials are added into the mix, we have all the necessary ingredients for the formation and survival of archaeological sites that allow us to reconstruct past animal behavior. Archaeology is an intrinsically interdisciplinary science, and adding ancient animal tool use to its research targets has been a satisfying—and even intuitive—step.

By chance, the recent rise of primate archaeology has coincided with the release of a new series of *Planet of the Apes* films. In them, our great ape relatives develop crude technologies that nonetheless rapidly surpass those known from wild animals in the real world. Even a simple composite spear, joining a sharp head to a separate shaft, requires a cognitive leap that appears absent in modern wild ape tools. Controlled use of fire and the wearing of jewelry are similarly extraordinary attributes of apes in these films, with no real-life examples of these behaviors known outside the human lineage.

But the technological apes we see on screen do not seem completely outlandish. They are even plausible. Western chimpanzees fashion simple, one-piece spears to attack smaller primates, just as capuchins do for lizards. William McGrew of the University of St. Andrews in Scotland, the most knowledgeable observer of chimp tool use and an early advocate for primate archaeology, once reported on an eastern chimp wearing a "necklace" made of knotted monkey skin. What else may take place when humans and their notebooks are not following these animals?

Human archaeology has emerged as a reliable source of insights into our development and diversity, a result of the efforts of thousands of scientists and billions of dollars over more than a century. As a reward for this effort, we now have millions of years of material culture that can act as a scaffold for our evolutionary speculations and scenarios. We are only at the starting line for the work to build a similar structure for nonhuman animals. But with an open mind, who knows what we might find? It is time to get digging that next square hole.

Referenced

Archaeological Excavation of Wild Macaque Stone Tools. Michael Haslam et al. in Journal of Human Evolution, Vol. 96, pages 134-138; July 2016.

Pre-Columbian Monkey Tools. Michael Haslam et al. in Current Biology, Vol. 26, No. 13, pages R521-R522; July 2016.

Wild Monkeys Flake Stone Tools. Tomos Proffitt et al. in Nature, Vol. 539, pages 85-88; November 2016.

About the Author

Michael Haslam is an independent researcher based in London. His work focuses on the evolution of technology in humans and other species.

Early Butchers Used Small Stone Scalpels

By Christopher Intagliata

Homo erectus used hand axes to butcher elephants and other game. But a new study suggests they also used finer, more sophisticated blades. Christopher Intagliata reports.

Archaeologists have spent a lot of time analyzing the *flashiest* objects recovered at ancient sites. But now they're giving a second look at the *waste* and finding that it, too, tells tales about a culture. For example, 8,000-year-old poop recently revealed parasitic infections among people who lived in settlements versus their hunter-gatherer counterparts. And now archaeologists have examined another overlooked artifact–small stone flakes, typically thought to be by-products from the production of tools like hand axes and cleavers.

"It was not easy to convince the scientific community that there is value to studying these items, because they were regarded just as waste."

Ran Barkai, an archaeologist at Tel Aviv University. His team studied 283 stone flakes found in Israel, at a site inhabited by our *Homo erectus* relatives, half a million years ago.

They found evidence of use–like small fractures–along the edges of the inch-long flakes. But they also discovered bits of bone and flesh still sticking to the tiny blades–flesh that could have come from *elephants*. The big mammals were much more widespread back then and were a prominent source of protein for early humans in that area.

The team then tested *replicas* of the flakes to butcher wild boars and deer and sheep. And they concluded that such tools would have been really useful to ancient hunters–for skinning hides, filleting meat and scraping every bit of nutrition out of an animal. Details and photos of the small scalpels are in the journal *Scientific Reports*.

Barkai also says the tiny flakes suggest these people were more sophisticated than they get credit for. "Walmarts were nonexistent at the time. So they had to do everything by themselves. And the fact that they survived and thrived for hundreds of thousands of years tells me they were highly capable, highly intelligent. I'm sure they were no less capable than us. And if not for their intelligence, we wouldn't be here."

–Christopher Intagliata

[The above text is a transcript of this podcast.]

Stone Age String Strengthens Case for Neandertal Smarts

By Kate Wong

Fibers twisted together to form string might not sound like bleeding-edge technology. But with string, or cordage, one can make bags, nets, rope and clothing. We use it to lace our shoes, floss our teeth, suspend bridges, transmit electrical power–the list goes on and on. Naturally, archaeologists have been eager to trace the origins of this pivotal innovation. But doing so is a difficult business because ancient string was made from perishable materials that have mostly been lost to time.

Now archaeologists who have been excavating a rock shelter in France have recovered a fragment of string that could push back the known record of this technology by tens of thousands of years. What is more, the artifact appears to be the handiwork of Neandertals, adding to mounting evidence that our extinct cousins were cleverer than they have been given credit for.

Until recently, the oldest direct evidence of string technology came from a site called Ohalo II in Israel and the famed Lascaux Cave in France. The bits of preserved string found at these sites date to 19,000 and 17,000 years ago, respectively, and were made by early members of our own species. But there were hints that fiber technology might have deeper roots in *Homo sapiens* culture. Impressions of woven fabric have been found on fired clay from sites in Moravia dating back as far as 28,000 years ago. And ivory artifacts from sites in Germany that may have been used for spinning plant fibers are up to 40,000 years old.

In 2013 archaeologist Bruce Hardy of Kenyon College and his colleagues reported that they had found plant fibers that looked as though they had been twisted to form string in excavations at the Abri du Maras rock shelter in southeastern France, which once harbored Neandertals. But with only individual fibers to go on, as opposed to actual string showing them twisted together, the case was far from airtight.

In the new study, published today in *Scientific Reports*, Hardy and his co-authors describe a 6.2-millimeter-long fragment of string that their team found at the same rock shelter –in a layer dated to between 52,000 and 41,000 years ago, when Neandertals occupied the site. Analyses of the fragment show that it is made of fibers that were probably harvested from the inner bark of a conifer tree. The fibers were twisted clockwise to form yarn, and then three lengths of the yarn were twisted in the opposite direction to make string.

Exactly what the string was used for is uncertain. But it was found adhering to a sharp-edged stone flake, leading the authors to suggest that it might have been applied to attach the flake to a handle of some sort. Alternatively, they suppose, the string might have had nothing to do with the stone flake and instead have been part of a net or bag.

Specific usage aside, the manufacture of the string attests to cognitive sophistication in Neandertals, Hardy and his colleagues contend. Harvesting the fibers would have required intimate knowledge of the growth and seasonality of the trees. And producing string after one has the raw material is itself mentally demanding, requiring the maker to keep track of multiple, sequential operations at the same time. Considering these findings, along with discoveries of different advanced technologies and even art at other Neandertal sites, "it is difficult to see how we can regard [Neandertals] as anything other than the cognitive equals of modern humans," Hardy and his co-authors write.

Outside researchers are intrigued by the new work. "I'm not 100 percent convinced" that the find is, in fact, a piece of string, says archaeologist Marie Soressi of Leiden University in the Netherlands, noting that she finds the photographs that accompany the team's paper "difficult to understand." But the new work constitutes "by far the best evidence" that the Neandertals at Abri du Maras made string, she says.

In Soressi's view, the most exciting aspect of the study is not what it demonstrates about Neandertals' sophistication—we already know their technology was very complex, she observes—but instead what it reveals about preservation. The previous record holder for the oldest known string remains came from a site that had been exposed to groundwater for a long time. Such waterlogged sites tend to preserve perishable materials, such as plant fibers, quite well. The new work by Hardy and his colleagues "supports the idea that microscopic residues of strings are preserved in nonwaterlogged rock-shelter deposits of Neandertal age," Soressi observes. Perishable objects account for much of the material culture of humans. Yet most of what archaeologists know about prehistoric humans, including the Neandertals, comes from the durable bones and stone tools they left behind. The ability to recover traces of the perishable materials our ancient predecessors used stands to reveal their lives in a whole new light.

About the Author

Kate Wong is a senior editor for evolution and ecology at Scientific American.

Is This Going to Be a Stand-Up Fight, Sir, or Another Sloth Hunt?

By Riley Black

White Sands National Monument is a strange place. Hemmed in by military installations, it's the only national park I know of that's had to cope with "errant missiles." The park also tangles with the ravenous appetites of African oryx, introduced as game animals in the 1960s and finding New Mexico perfect to their tastes. But perhaps the oddest aspect of this remote park is what remains of its distant past. During the Pleistocene, over 12,000 years ago, mammoths, saber-toothed cats, and other megafauna left their footprints around an enormous, ancient lake. Those traces remain, weathering out of the arid desert flats, and, among this fantastic aggregation of tracks, paleontologists have what was either an Ice Age hunt or the Pleistocene equivalent of cow tipping.

The tracks, described by park naturalist David Bustos and colleagues, were found near the margin of one of the park's alkali flats. About 30,000 years ago, this now-desolate place was part of Paleo-Lake Otero. That water source not only attracted life, but provided just the right conditions for their footfalls to be preserved. In this case, a strange interaction between prehistoric people and a giant ground sloth.

Seeing the tracks together, I had to chuckle a little. Over a century ago, giant ground sloth tracks found in Carson City, Nevada made news because their crescent shapes looked like the footprints of a human giant. If the White Sands National Monument tracks at the center of the new paper had been found earlier, perhaps Mark Twain would have been lampooning these fossils rather than those found at the Carson City prison. As it stands, though, the scientific analysis has something even more spectacular to share. The tracks of the giant ground sloth and the Pleistocene people show how these Ice Age inhabitants reacted to each other.

Trace fossils are recordings of prehistoric behavior. This is true whether paleontologists are looking at a single footfall or an entire trackway. But finding interactions between organisms—and particularly different species—is rare, particularly in this case where humans have often been implicated in the demise of charismatic mammals like the shuffling ground sloths. (Giant sloth bones found in Uruguay supposedly show signs of cut marks made by humans, for example, but the evidence is disputed.) The tracks present a few fleeting moments of Pleistocene life.

So what happened? Sussing out the story isn't as simple as just following one foot in front of the other. Determining the window in which tracks were formed is critical to determining interactions. In this case, there are over a hundred sloth and human tracks representing several individuals of each group. This wasn't a gang of humans running up to a single sloth. It seems that the prehistoric people either harassed a group of sloths or bothered multiple sloths in close succession. Whenever the human tracks come in close proximity to the sloth tracks, Bustos and colleagues write, the sloth traces seem to show evasive and defensive behavior. There are even tracks that look like places where the sloths stood up on their hind legs into a defensive posture similar to what giant anteaters do today.

The question is what these Pleistocene people were doing. Bustos and coauthors are right that sloths were not to be trifled with. The megamammals had thick skin, toughened further by pebbles of bone, and each of these mammals had burly arms tipped in sharp claws that "gave them a lethal reach and clear advantage in close-quarter encounters." Hunting giant sloths would have been a fool's errand, if that's even what these people were doing.

There's no giant sloth body at the end of the trackways. Nor are there tracks and traces showing a sloth being felled. Tools and weapons prehistoric people would have used are also absent from the site. We know the people got close enough to bother the sloths, but there's no direct evidence for hunting. Only the assumption that prehistoric people might have done so. But there's another set of tracks that speaks to an alternative, even if it's almost impossible to confirm.

Human tracks don't just surround the sloth tracks. Some of the human tracks fall *within* the giant sloth footprints. Ease of passage—like a person following a game trail—doesn't make sense. This was a lake margin, not a closed-in habitat. And, as Bustos and colleagues write, it would have actually been a little uncomfortable for the person to do this. Their stride length was shorter than that of the sloth, so they would have needed to take an unnatural gait to match up with the prints—just like I do with some dinosaur trackways out in the desert. That kind of ichnological fun might be the key to a scenario that contrasts with the violent confrontations depicted in news reports on this paper.

"It is possible that the behavior was playful," Bustos and colleagues write, the Pleistocene person following in the footsteps of the sloths just because they could. Maybe the entire encounter was a matter of Pleistocene fun or even a dare, harassing the sloths more for entertainment than food. Admittedly, this is an untestable hypothesis. The tracks don't testify to this possibility. But neither should hunting be taken as the default in the absence of evidence to support it. Do the White Sands tracks represent an unsuccessful hunt? Maybe. But it's just as likely that they confirm the long history of people being jerks to animals.

The views expressed are those of the author(s) and are not necessarily those of Scientific American.

About the Author

Riley Black, who formerly wrote under the name Brian Switek, is the author of Skeleton Keys *and* My Beloved Brontosaurus. *She lives in Salt Lake City, Utah.*

The Origins of Creativity

By Heather Pringle

Unsigned and undated, inventory number 779 hangs behind thick glass in the Louvre's brilliantly lit Salle des États. A few minutes after the stroke of nine each morning, except for Tuesdays when the museum remains closed, Parisians and tourists, art lovers and curiosity seekers begin flooding into the room. As their hushed voices blend into a steady hivelike hum, some crane for the best view; others stretch their arms urgently upward, clicking cell-phone cameras. Most, however, tilt forward, a look of rapt wonder on their faces, as they study one of humanity's most celebrated creations: the *Mona Lisa*, by Leonardo da Vinci.

Completed in the early 16th century, the *Mona Lisa* possesses a mysterious, otherworldly beauty quite unlike any portrait that came before it. To produce such a painting, Leonardo developed a new artistic technique he called *sfumato*, or "smoke." Over a period of several years he applied translucent glazes in delicate films—some no more than the thickness of a red blood cell—to the painting, most likely with the sensitive tip of his finger. Gradually stacking as many as 30 of these films one on top of another, Leonardo subtly softened lines and color gradations until it seemed as if the entire composition lay behind a veil of smoke.

The *Mona Lisa* is clearly a work of inventive genius, a masterpiece that stands alongside the music of Mozart, the jewels of Fabergé, the choreography of Martha Graham, and other such classics. But these renowned works are only the grandest manifestations of a trait that has long seemed part of our human hardwiring: the ability to create something new and desirable, the knack of continually improving designs and technologies—from the latest zero-emissions cars made in Japan to the sleekly engineered Falcon 9 rockets from SpaceX. Modern humans, says Christopher S. Henshilwood, an archaeologist at the Universities of Bergen in Norway and the Witwatersrand, Johannesburg, in

South Africa, "are inventors of note. We advance and experiment with technology constantly."

Just how we came by this seemingly infinite capacity to create is the subject of intense scientific study: we were not always such whirlwinds of invention. Although our human lineage emerged in Africa around 6 million years ago, early family members left behind little visible record of innovation for nearly 3.4 million years, suggesting that they obtained plant and animal foods by hand, with tools such as digging or jabbing sticks that did not preserve. Then, at some point, wandering hominins started flaking water-worn cobblestones with hammerstones to produce cutting tools. That was an act of astonishing ingenuity, to be sure, but a long plateau followed–during which very little seems to have happened on the creativity front. Our early ancestors apparently knapped the same style of handheld, multipurpose hand ax for 1.6 million years, with only minor tweaks to the template. "Those tools are really kind of stereotypical," says Sally McBrearty, an archaeologist at the University of Connecticut.

So when did the human mind begin churning with new ideas for technology and art? Until recently, most researchers pointed to the start of the Upper Paleolithic period 40,000 years ago, when *Homo sapiens* embarked on what seemed a sudden, wondrous invention spree in Europe: fashioning shell-bead necklaces, adorning cave walls with geometric signs and paintings of Ice Age animals, and carving and knapping a wide variety of new stone and bone tools. The finds prompted a popular theory proposing that a random genetic mutation at around that time had spurred a sudden leap in human cognition, igniting a creative "big bang."

New evidence, however, has cast grave doubt on the mutation theory. Over the past decade or so archaeologists have uncovered far older evidence of art and advanced technology, suggesting that the human capacity to cook up new ideas evolved much earlier than previously thought–even before the emergence of *H. sapiens* 200,000 years ago. Yet although our capacity for creativity sparked early on, it then smoldered for millennia before finally catching fire in our species in Africa and Europe. The evidence seems to indicate that our power of innovation did not burst into existence fully formed late in our evolutionary history but rather gained steam over hundreds of thousands of years, fueled by a complex mix of biological and social factors.

Exactly when did humankind begin thinking outside the box, and what factors converged to ultimately fan our brilliant creative fire? Understanding this scenario requires following a detective story composed of several strands of evidence, starting with the one showing that the biological roots of our creativity date back much further than scientists once thought.

Mother of Invention

Archaeologists have long viewed the use of symbols as the single most important indicator of modern human cognition, in large part because it attests to a capacity for language—a hallmark human trait. Thus, the geometric signs and the spectacular cave art of the Upper Paleolithic clearly signal the presence of people who thought as we do. But more recently, experts have begun searching for hints of other kinds of modern behavior and its antecedents in the archaeological record—and coming up with fascinating clues.

Archaeologist Lyn Wadley of the University of the Witwatersrand, Johannesburg, has spent much of her career studying ancient cognition, research that led her in the 1990s to open excavations at Sibudu Cave, some 40 kilometers north of Durban, South Africa. At that same site, about five years ago, she and her team discovered a layer of strange, white, fibrous plant material there. To Wadley, the pale, brittle mash looked like ancient bedding—rushes and other plants that later people often scattered on the ground for sitting and sleeping on. But the layer could also have formed from wind-borne leaf litter. The only way to tell one from the other was to encase the entire layer in a protective plaster jacket and take it back to the laboratory. "It took us three weeks to make all that plaster,"

Wadley recounts, "and I was really grumpy the whole time. I kept wondering, 'Am I wasting three weeks in the field?'"

But Wadley's gamble paid off richly. In 2011 she and her colleagues reported in *Science* that Sibudu's occupants selected leaves from just one of many woody species in the area to make bedding 77,000 years ago—nearly 50,000 years earlier than previously reported examples. What most surprised Wadley, however, was the occupants' sophisticated knowledge of the local vegetation. Analysis showed that the chosen leaves came from *Cryptocarya woodii*, a tree containing traces of natural insecticides and larvicides effective against the mosquitoes that carry deadly disease today. "And that's very handy to have in your bedding, particularly if you live near a river," Wadley observes.

The creative minds at Sibudu did not stop there, however. They most likely devised snares to capture small antelopes, whose remains litter the site, and crafted bows and arrows to bring down more dangerous prey, judging from the sizes, shapes and wear patterns of several stone points from the cave. Moreover, Sibudu's hunters concocted various valuable new chemical compounds. By shooting a high-energy beam of charged particles at dark residues on stone points from the cave, Wadley's team detected multi-ingredient glues that once fastened the points to wood hafts. She and her colleagues then set about experimentally replicating these adhesives, mixing ocher particles of different sizes with plant gums and heating the mixtures over wood fires. Publishing the results in *Science*, the team concluded that Sibudu's occupants were very likely "competent chemists, alchemists and pyrotechnologists" by 70,000 years ago.

Elsewhere in southern Africa, researchers have recently turned up traces of many other early inventions. The hunter-gatherers who inhabited Blombos Cave between 100,000 and 72,000 years ago, for example, engraved patterns on chunks of ocher; fashioned bone awls, perhaps for tailoring hide clothing; adorned themselves with strands of shimmering shell beads; and created an artists' studio where they ground red ocher and stored it in the earliest known containers, made from abalone shells. Farther west, at the site of Pinnacle Point, people engineered the stone they worked with 164,000 years ago, heating a low-grade, local rock known as silcrete over a controlled fire to transform it into a lustrous, easily knappable material. "We are seeing behaviors that we didn't even dream about 10 years ago," Henshilwood remarks.

Moreover, technological ingenuity was not the sole preserve of modern humans: other hominins possessed a creative streak, too. In northern Italy a research team headed by University of Florence archaeologist Paul Peter Anthony Mazza discovered that our near kin, the Neandertals, who first emerged in Europe some 300,000 years ago, concocted a birch bark–tar glue to fasten stone flakes to wood handles, fabricating hafted tools some 200,000 years ago. Likewise, a study published in 2012 in Science concluded that stone points from the site of Kathu Pan 1 in South Africa once formed the lethal tips of 500,000-year-old spears, presumably belonging to *Homo heidelbergensis*, the last common ancestor of Neandertals and *H. sapiens*. And at Wonderwerk Cave in South Africa, an ancient layer containing plant ash and bits of burned bone suggests that an even earlier hominin, *Homo erectus*, learned to kindle fires for warmth and protection from predators as early as 1 million years ago.

Even our very distant ancestors were capable on occasion of coining new ideas. At two sites near the Kada Gona River in Ethiopia, a team led by paleoanthropologist Sileshi Semaw of Indiana University Bloomington found stone tools—2.6-million-year-old choppers knapped by *Australopithecus garhi* or one of its contemporaries, likely for stripping meat from animal carcasses. Such tools look crude to us, a far cry from the smartphones, laptops and tablets of today. "But when the world consisted solely of naturally formed objects, the capacity to imagine something and turn it into a reality may well have seemed almost magical," wrote cognitive scientist Liane Gabora of the University of British Columbia and psychologist Scott Barry Kaufman, now at the University of Pennsylvania, in a chapter appearing in *The Cambridge Handbook of Creativity* (Cambridge University Press, 2010).

Cognition and Creation

Yet impressive as these early flashes of creativity are, the great disparity in the depth and breadth of innovation between modern humans and our distant forebears demands an explanation. What changes in the brain set our kind apart from our predecessors? By poring over three-dimensional scans of ancient hominin braincases and by examining the brains of our nearest living evolutionary kin–chimpanzees and bonobos, whose ancestors branched off from our lineage some 6 million years ago–researchers are beginning to unlock this puzzle. Their data show just how extensively human gray matter evolved over time.

Generally speaking, natural selection favored large brains in humans. Whereas our australopithecine kin possessed an estimated mean cranial capacity of 450 cubic centimeters, roughly that of some chimpanzees, *H. erectus* more than doubled that capacity by 1.6 million years ago, with a mean of 930 cubic centimeters. And by 100,000 years ago *H. sapiens* had a mean capacity of 1,330 cubic centimeters. Inside this spacious braincase, an estimated 100 billion neurons processed information and transmitted it along nearly 165,000 kilometers of myelinated nerve fibers and across some 0.15 quadrillion synapses. "And if you look at what this correlates with in the archaeological record," says Dean Falk, a paleoneurologist at Florida State University, "there does seem to be an association between brain size and technology or intellectual productivity."

But size was not the only major change over time. At the University of California, San Diego, biological anthropologist Katerina Semendeferi studies a part of the brain known as the prefrontal cortex, which appears to orchestrate thought and action to accomplish goals. Examining this region in modern humans and in both chimpanzees and bonobos, Semendeferi and her colleagues discovered that several key subareas underwent a major reorganization during hominin evolution. Brodmann area 10, for example–which is implicated in bringing plans to fruition and organizing sensory input–nearly doubled in volume after chimpanzees and bonobos branched off from our human lineage. Moreover, the horizontal spaces between neurons in this subarea widened by nearly 50 percent, creating more room for axons and dendrites. "This means that you can have more complicated connections and ones that go farther away, so you can get more complex and more synthetic communication between neurons," Falk comments.

Pinpointing just how a bigger, reorganized brain spurred creativity is a tricky business. But Gabora thinks that psychological studies of creative people today supply a key clue. Such individuals are excellent woolgatherers, she explains. When tackling a problem, they first let their minds wander, allowing one memory or thought to spontaneously conjure up another. This free association encourages analogies and gives rise to thoughts that break out of the box. Then, as these individuals settle on a vague idea for a solution, they switch to a more analytic mode of thought. "They zero in on only the most relevant properties," Gabora says, and they start refining an idea to make it workable.

In all likelihood, Gabora notes, a bigger brain led to a greater ability to free-associate. More stimuli could be encoded in a brain made up of many billions of neurons. In addition, more neurons could participate in the encoding of a particular episode, leading to a finer-grained memory and more potential routes for associating one stimulus with another. Imagine, Gabora says, that a hominin brushes against a spiny shrub and sharp thorns tear its flesh. An australopithecine might encode this episode very simply—as a minor pain and as an identifiable feature of the shrub. But *H. erectus*, with its larger assembly of neurons, could conceivably encode many aspects of the episode. Then, when this hominin begins hunting, its need to kill prey might activate all memory locations encoding torn flesh, bringing to mind the encounter with the sharp pointed thorns. That memory, in turn, could inspire a fresh idea for a weapon: a spear with a sharp pointed tip.

But large-brained hominins could not afford to linger too long in an associative state in which one thing immediately reminded them of a flood of other things, both important and inconsequential. Their survival depended mostly on analytic thought—the default mode. So our ancestors had to develop a way of switching smoothly from one mode to another by subtly altering concentrations of dopamine and other neurotransmitters.

Gabora now hypothesizes that *H. sapiens* needed tens of thousands of years to fine-tune this mechanism before they could reap the full creative benefit of their large brains, and she and her students are testing these ideas on an artificial neural network. Through a computer model, they simulate the brain's ability to switch between the analytic and associative mode to see how it could help someone break out of a cognitive rut and see things in a new way. "Just having more neurons isn't enough," Gabora asserts. "You have to be able to make use of all that extra gray matter." Once that final piece of the biological puzzle fell into place—perhaps a little more than 100,000 years ago—the ancestral mind was a virtual tinder box, awaiting the right social circumstances to burst into flame.

Building on Brilliance

In the autumn of 1987 two researchers, both then at the University of Zurich—Christophe and Hedwige Boesch—observed a behavior they had never seen before in a group of chimpanzees foraging for food in Tai National Park in Ivory Coast. Near a ground nest belonging to a species of driver ants, a female stopped and picked up a twig. She dipped one end into the loose soil covering the nest's entrance and waited for the colony's soldier ants to attack. When the dark swarm had advanced nearly 10 centimeters up the twig, the female chimpanzee plucked it from the nest and deftly rolled it toward her mouth, snacking on the ants. She then repeated the process until she had eaten her fill.

Chimpanzees are highly adept at using a wide range of tools—cracking open nuts with stones, sponging up water from tree hollows with leaves and unearthing nutritious plant roots with digging sticks. But they seem unable to build on this knowledge or to craft ever more advanced technology. "Chimps can show other chimps how to hunt termites," Henshilwood says, "but they don't improve on it, they don't say, 'Let's do it with a different kind of probe'—they just do the same thing over and over." Modern humans, in contrast, suffer from no such limitations. Indeed, we daily take the ideas of others and put our own twist on them, adding one modification after another, until we end up with something new and very complex. No one individual, for example, came up with all the intricate technology embedded in a laptop computer: such technological achievements arise from the creative insights of generations of inventors.

Anthropologists call this knack of ours cultural ratcheting. It requires, first and foremost, the ability to pass on knowledge from one individual to another or from one generation to the next, until someone comes along with an idea for an improvement.

In a 2012 study published in *Science* by Lewis Dean, a behavioral primatologist at the University of St. Andrews in Scotland, and four colleagues revealed why human beings can do this and chimpanzees and capuchin monkeys cannot. Dean and his team designed an experimental puzzle box, with three sequential and incrementally difficult levels: then they presented it to groups of chimps in Texas, capuchin monkeys in France and nursery schoolchildren in England. Only one of the 55 nonhuman primates—a chimp—reached the highest level after more than 30 hours of trying. The children, however, fared far better. Unlike the groups of monkeys, the children worked collaboratively—talking among themselves, offering encouragement and showing one another the right way to do things. After two and a half hours, 15 of the 35 children had reached level three.

Equipped with these social skills and cognitive abilities, our ancestors could readily transmit knowledge to others—a key prerequisite for cultural ratcheting. Yet something else was needed to propel the ratcheting process and push *H. sapiens* to new creative heights in Africa some 90,000 to 60,000 years ago and in Europe 40,000 years ago. Mark Thomas, an evolutionary geneticist at

University College London, thinks this push came from demography. His premise is simple. The larger a hunter-gatherer group is, the greater the chances are that one member will dream up an idea that could advance a technology. Moreover, individuals in a large group who frequently rubbed shoulders with neighbors had a better chance of learning a new innovation than those in small, isolated groups. "It's not how smart you are," Thomas says. "It's how well connected you are."

To test these ideas, Thomas and two colleagues developed a computer model to simulate the effects of demography on the ratcheting process. With genetic data from modern Europeans, the team estimated the size of modern human populations in Europe at the beginning of the Upper Paleolithic, when evidence of human creativity started to spike, and calculated the population density. Then the researchers examined African populations over time, simulating their growth and patterns of migratory activity. Their model showed that African populations reached the same density as the early Upper Paleolithic Europeans around 101,000 years ago, just before innovation began to take off in sub-Saharan regions, according to the archaeological record. It also showed that large social networks actively spur human creativity.

Archaeological evidence published in 2012 in *Nature* sheds light on the tech renaissance that followed the rise of population density in southern Africa. Some 71,000 years ago at Pinnacle Point, *H. sapiens* devised and passed down to others a complex technological recipe to make lightweight stone blades for projectile weapons–cooking silcrete to a specific temperature to improve its flaking qualities, knapping the finished material into blades little more than a couple of centimeters long, and mounting them on wood or bone shafts with homemade glue. "Like viruses," note archaeologists Fiona Coward of Bournemouth University and Matt Grove of the University of Liverpool in England in a paper published in 2011 in *PaleoAnthropology*, "cultural innovations need very particular social conditions to spread–most notably... large connected populations who can 'infect' one another."

Which brings us to the jostling, teeming, intimately linked world we live in today. Never before have humans crowded together in such massive cities, accessing vast realms of knowledge with a click of the keyboard and sharing new concepts, new blueprints and designs across the sprawling social networks of the World Wide Web. And never before has the pace of innovation accelerated so dramatically, filling our lives with new fashions, new electronics, new cars, new music, new architecture.

Half a millennium after Leonardo da Vinci conceived of his most celebrated work, we marvel at his inventive genius—a genius built on the countless ideas and inventions of a lineage of artists stretching back into the Paleolithic past. And even now a new crop of artists gaze at the Mona Lisa with an eye to turning it into something fresh and dazzlingly creative. The human chain of invention remains unbroken, and in our superbly connected world, our singular talent to create races on ahead of us.

Referenced

Middle Stone Age Bedding Construction and Settlement Patterns at Sibudu, South Africa. Lyn Wadley et al. in *Science*, Vol. 334, pages 1388–1391; December 9, 2011.

Hominin Paleoneurology: Where Are We Now? Dean Falk in *Progress in Brain Research*, Vol. 195, pages 255–272; 2012.

About the Author

Heather Pringle is a Canadian science writer and a contributing correspondent for Science.

Mind Your "Fs" and "Vs": Agriculture May Have Shaped Both Human Jaws and Language

By Anne Pycha

The organs of speech are the same for all people, or so linguists have typically assumed. But it turns out that may not be true—in fact, what you eat can change how you talk.

The conventional wisdom held in the field of historical linguistics is the vocal apparatus of human beings has remained fixed since the emergence of *Homo sapiens* some 200,000 years ago. As a consequence, all humans, both ancient and modern peoples, possess the same basic capacity to produce speech sounds. But recent evidence from several studies in paleoanthropology has upended these assumptions by suggesting the way we eat can actually alter jaw anatomy. And according to research just published in *Science*, the consequences for the way we speak have been profound.

The lead authors of the study, Damián Blasi and Steven Moran of the University of Zurich along with colleagues, became intrigued by fossil evidence showing the form of the human jaw had changed in our species's relatively recent evolutionary past. Among hunter-gatherers of the Paleolithic period, adults' upper and lower teeth aligned to form a flat line, the top ones resting directly on the bottom set. Scientists attribute that configuration primarily to tooth wear brought about by chewing hard foods, such as unmilled grains or seeds. With the advent of agriculture in the post-Neolithic period, however, the upper teeth protruded over and above the lower teeth, presumably due to the reduced challenge of consuming soft foods such as porridge and cheese.

These findings suggest not only that the cultural shift that gave rise to agriculture occasioned a shift in human anatomy. It also appears to have introduced new speech sounds known as labiodentals—the "f" and "v," for instance. Blasi and Moran's study furnishes evidence that adopting the signature foodstuffs of sedentary society ultimately allowed us to mouth words like "farro" and "verbalize" by raising the lower lip and bringing it into contact with the upper teeth. Their research group conducted biomechanical simulations of this movement using two different virtual jaws to calculate the muscular effort involved. Their results showed, compared with the protruding bites, the flat bite configurations required substantially more effort to produce a labiodental.

Linguists had already established that articulatory effort can affect the fate of a phoneme, so Blasi and Moran's team speculated that labiodentals would have been less likely to emerge among any population with flat bites, such as Paleolithic humans, or even modern humans who eat harder foods. To test this hypothesis, they analyzed databases of the world's consonants and showed contemporary hunter–gatherer languages contain only a fraction of the labiodental sounds that food-producer languages do. Of course, food preparation techniques are merely a stand-in for actual bite configurations. To make the link more explicit, the researchers separately analyzed hunter–gatherer societies in Greenland, southern Africa and Australia, where flat bites have been explicitly documented. In line with their hypothesis, results turned up relatively few languages with labiodentals among these populations. When one of these sounds appeared, it was usually borrowed from other languages.

As a final piece of support for their argument, Blasi and Moran's team examined sound changes in Indo-European languages over time. They used a nontraditional technique called stochastic character mapping, which calculates the numerical probability a sound existed in a language at a particular point in time. Results showed labiodental sounds were extremely unlikely in almost all branches of Indo-European, until anytime from 6,000 to 4,000 years ago. After that period, which coincides with the introduction of soft foods, the probability of these sounds showed a notable increase.

The take-home message: "we can't take for granted that spoken languages sound the same today as they did in the distant past,"

Moran says. "This means in particular that the set of speech sounds we use has not necessarily remained stable since the emergence of our species, but rather the immense diversity of speech sounds that we find today is the product of a complex interplay of factors involving biological change and cultural evolution."

Not everyone is convinced of the arguments put forth in the new study. Israel Hershkovitz of Tel Aviv University points out many factors besides tooth wear can affect bite configurations. Also, tooth wear occurs gradually and does not fully affect bite dynamics until adulthood. Given the relatively short life expectancy of prehistoric hunter–gatherers, he says, it seems unlikely this anatomical trait could have affected language evolution.

To other observers, Blasi and Moran's study, along with others in recent years, reflects a paradigm shift in historical linguistics. "This paper revives an idea that linguists probably abandoned out of a natural apprehension–the danger of verging on ideas that could be interpreted as racist–which arises whenever anatomical differences between populations are proposed to play a role in any aspect of language or cognition," says Andrew Garrett of the University of California, Berkeley, who was not involved in the study. "Today, however, there is clear evidence that individual anatomical, physiological and perceptual differences do play some role in linguistic differences."

The Cultural Origins of Language

By Christine Kenneally

Dolphins name one another, and they click and whistle about their lives or the dangers posed by sharks and humans. They also pass on useful bits of know-how from mother to child, such as how to catch fish or how to flee. If they had language in the same sense that we do, however, they would not only pass down little bits of information but also aggregate them into a broad body of knowledge about the world. Over the span of generations clever practices, complex knowledge and technology based on two, three or several components would develop. Dolphins would have history–and with history, they would learn about the journeys and ideas of other dolphin groups, and any one individual could inherit a fragment of language, say, a story or poem, from another individual who had lived hundreds of years before. That dolphin would be touched, through language, by the wisdom of another dolphin, who was in every other way long gone.

Only humans can perform this spectacular time-traveling feat, just as only humans can penetrate the stratosphere or bake strawberry shortcake. Because we have language, we have modern technology, culture, art and scientific inquiry. We have the ability to ask questions such as, Why is language unique to humans? Despite the accumulated genius we inherit when we learn to speak or sign, we have yet to work out a good answer. But a diverse group of brain scientists, linguists, animal researchers and geneticists are tackling the question–so we are much closer to a real understanding than ever before.

An Unanswerable Question

That language is uniquely human has been assumed for a long time. But trying to work out exactly how and why that is the case has been weirdly taboo. In the 1860s the Société de Linguistique de Paris banned discussion about the evolution of language, and the Philological Society of London banned it in the 1870s. They may have wanted to clamp down on unscientific speculation, or perhaps it was a political move–either way, more than a century's worth of nervousness about the subject followed. Noam Chomsky, the extraordinarily influential linguist at the Massachusetts Institute of Technology, was, for decades, rather famously disinterested in language evolution, and his attitude had a chilling effect on the field. Attending an undergraduate linguistics class in Melbourne, Australia, in the early 1990s, I asked my lecturer how language evolved. I was told that linguists did not ask the question, because it was not really possible to answer it.

Luckily, just a few years later, scholars from different disciplines began to grapple with the question in earnest. The early days of serious research in language evolution unearthed a perplexing paradox: Language is plainly, obviously, uniquely human. It consists of wildly complicated interconnecting sets of rules for combining sounds and words and sentences to create meaning. If other animals had a system that was the same, we would likely recognize it. The problem is that after looking for a considerable amount of time and with a wide range of methodological approaches, we cannot seem to find anything unique in ourselves–either in the human genome or in the human brain–that explains language.

To be sure, we have found biological features that are both unique to humans and important for language. For example, humans are the only primates to have voluntary control of their larynx: it puts us at risk of choking, but it allows us to articulate speech. But the equipment that seems to be designed for language never fully explains its enormous complexity and utility.

It seems more and more that the paradox is not inherent in language but in how we look at it. For a long time we have been in love with the idea of a sudden, explosive transformation that changed mere apes into us. The idea of metamorphosis has gone hand in hand with a list of equally dramatic ideas. For example: that language is a wholly discrete trait that has little in common with other kinds of mental activity; that language is the evolutionary adaptation that changed everything; and that language is wired into humanity's DNA. We have looked for a critical biological event that brought complex language into existence around 50,000 years ago.

Findings from genetics, cognitive science and brain sciences are now converging in a different place. It looks like language is not a brilliant adaptation. Nor is it encoded in the human genome or the inevitable output of our superior human brains. Instead language grows out of a platform of abilities, some of which are very ancient and shared with other animals and only some of which are more modern.

Talking to the Animals

Animal researchers were the first to challenge the definition of language as a discretely human attribute. As comparative psychologist Heidi Lyn has pointed out, the only way we can truly determine what is unique to human language is to explore the capacities of other animals. Interestingly, almost every time researchers have proposed that humans can do something that other animals cannot because humans have language, studies have shown that some animals can do some of those things, at least some of the time.

Take gestures, for example. Some are individual, but many are common to our language community and even to all humans. It is clear that language evolved as part of a communication system in which gesture also plays a role. But landmark work has shown that chimpanzees gesture in meaningful ways, too. Michael Tomasello, now emeritus at the Max Planck Institute for Evolutionary Anthropology in Leipzig, Germany, and his colleagues have shown that all species of great apes will wait until they have another ape's attention before they signal, and they repeat gestures that do not get the response they want. Chimpanzees slap the ground or clap their hands to get attention—and just as a belligerent human might raise a fist, they roll their arms over their head (normally a prelude to an attack) as a warning to rivals.

Even so, Tomasello's laboratory found that apes were very poor at understanding a human pointing gesture that conveyed information, such as, for example, the location of a hidden object. Does pointing—or rather the ability to fully understand it—represent a critical step in the evolution of language? The claim struck Lyn, who worked with bonobos that are now at the Ape Cognition and Conservation Initiative, as absurd. "My apes understood when I pointed to things all the time," she says. But when she set up pointing experiments with chimpanzees at the Yerkes National Primate Research Center at Emory University, she was surprised to find that the apes there did not understand her pointing well at all. Then she went back to the bonobos in her lab and tested them. All of them did.

The difference between the pointing apes and the nonpointing apes had nothing to do with biology, Lyn concluded. The bonobos had been taught to communicate with humans using simple visual symbols; the chimpanzees had not. "It's apes that haven't been around humans in the same way that can't follow pointing," she explains.

The fact that the bonobos were taught by humans has been used to dismiss their ability, according to Lyn, as if they were somehow tainted. Language research with parrots and dolphins and other animals has been discounted for the same reason. But Lyn argues that animals trained by humans provide valuable insights. If creatures with different brains and different bodies can learn some humanlike communicative skills, it means that language should not be defined as wholly human and disconnected from the rest of the animal world. Moreover, whereas language may be affected by biology, it is not necessarily determined by it. With the bonobos, it was culture, not biology, that made the critical difference.

Genetic Code

The list of abilities that were formerly thought to be a unique part of human language is actually quite long. It includes parts of language, such as words. Vervet monkeys use wordlike alarm calls to signal a specific kind of danger. Another crucial aspect is structure. Because we have syntax, we can produce an infinite number of novel sentences and meanings, and we can understand sentences that we have never heard before. Yet zebra finches have complicated structure in their songs, dolphins can understand differences in word order and even some monkeys in the wild seem to use one type of call to modify another. The list extends to types of cognition, such as theory of mind, which is the ability to infer others' mental states. Dolphins and chimpanzees are excellent at guessing what an interlocutor wants. Even the supposedly unique ability to think about numbers falls by the wayside–bees can understand the concept of zero, bees and rhesus monkeys can count to four, and cormorants used for fishing in China reportedly count to seven.

The list includes genes. The famous *FOXP2* gene, once called a language gene, is indeed a gene that affects language–when it is mutated, it disrupts articulation–but it performs other roles as well. There is no easy way to tease out the different effects. Genes are critical for understanding how language evolved, says Simon Fisher, a geneticist at the Max Planck Institute for Psycholinguistics in Nijmegen, the Netherlands, but "we have to think about what genes do." To put an incredibly complex process very briefly: genes code for proteins, which then affect cells, which may be brain cells that form neural circuits, and it is those circuits that are then responsible for behavior. "It may be that there is a network of genes that are important for syntactic processing or speaking proficiently," Fisher explains, "but there won't be a single gene that can magically code for a suite of abilities."

The list of no-longer-completely-unique human traits includes brain mechanisms, too. We are learning that neural circuits can develop multiple uses. One recent study showed that some neural circuits that underlie language learning may also be used for remembering lists or acquiring complicated skills, such as learning how to drive. Sure enough, the animal versions of the same circuits are used to solve similar problems, such as, in rats, navigating a maze.

Michael Arbib, a cognitive neuroscientist at the University of California, San Diego, notes that humans have created "a material and mental world of ever increasing complexity"–and yet whether a child is born into a world with the steam train or one with the iPhone, he or she can master some part of it without alterations in biology. "As far as we know," Arbib says, "the only type of brain on earth that can do that is the human brain." He emphasizes, however, that the brain is just one part of a complex system, which includes the body: "If dolphins had hands, maybe they could have evolved that world."

Indeed, making sense of the human world requires not only the brain in the body but also a group of brains interacting as part of the human social world. Arbib refers to this as an EvoDevoSocio approach. Biological evolution influences the development and learning of individuals, and individual learning shapes the evolution of culture; learning, in turn, can be shaped by culture. To understand language, the human brain has to be considered a part of those systems. The evolution of language was polycausal, Arbib says. No one switch was thrown: there were lots of switches. And it did not happen all at once but took a great deal of time.

Cultural Revolution

Culture also plays a critical role for Simon Kirby, a cognitive scientist who runs the Center for Language Evolution at the University of Edinburgh. From the beginning, Kirby was fascinated by the idea that not only is language something that we learn from others, but it is something that is passed down through generations of learners. What impact did the repeated act of learning have on language itself?

Kirby set out to test the question by fashioning a completely new method of exploring language evolution. Instead of looking at animals or humans, he built digital models of speakers, called agents, and fed them messy, random strings of language. His artificially intelligent agents had to learn the language from other agents, but then they had to teach other agents the language as well. Then

Kirby rolled over generations of learners and teachers to see how the language might change. He likened the task to the telephone game, where a message is passed on from one person to the next and so on, with the final message often ending up quite different from the original.

Kirby found that his digital agents had a tendency to produce more structure in their output than they had received in their input. Even though the strings of language he initially gave them were random, sometimes by chance a string might appear to be slightly ordered. Critically, the agents picked up on that structure, and they generalized it. "The learners, if you like, hallucinated structure in their input," Kirby says. Having seen structure where there was none, the agents then reproduced more structure in what they said.

The changes might be very tiny, Kirby notes, but over the generations "the process snowballs." Excitingly, not only did the agents' language begin to look more and more structured after many generations, the kind of structure that emerged looked like a simple version of that which occurs in natural human language. Subsequently Kirby tried a variety of different models and gave them different kinds of data, but he found that "the cumulative accretion of linguistic structure seemed to always happen no matter how we built the models." It was the crucible of learning over and over again that created the language itself.

Now Kirby is re-creating his digital experiments in real life with humans and even animals by getting them to repeat things that they learn. He is finding that structure indeed evolves in this way. One of the more thrilling implications of this discovery is how it helps to explain why we can never pin down the right single gene or mutation or brain circuit to explain language: it is just not there. Language seems to emerge out of a combination of biology, individual learning and the transmission of language from one individual to another. The three systems run at entirely different timescales, but when they interlock, something extraordinary happens: language is born.

In the short time since the field of language evolution has been active, researchers may have not reached the holy grail: a definitive event that explains language. But their work makes that quest somewhat beside the point. To be sure, language is probably the most unique biological trait on the planet. But it is much more fragile, fluky and contingent than anyone might have predicted.

Referenced

The First Word: The Search for the Origins of Language. Christine Kenneally. Viking, 2007.

How the Brain Got Language: The Mirror System Hypothesis. Michael A. Arbib. Oxford University Press, 2012.

Culture and Biology in the Origins of Linguistic Structure. Simon Kirby in *Psychonomic Bulletin & Review*, Vol. 24, No. 1, pages 118–137; February 2017.

The Question of Capacity: Why Enculturated and Trained Animals Have Much to Tell Us about the Evolution of Language. Heidi Lyn in *Psychonomic Bulletin & Review*, Vol. 24, No. 1, pages 85–90; February 2017.

About the Author

Christine Kenneally is an award-winning science journalist and author of two books, most recently The Invisible History of the Human Race *(Viking, 2014).*

An Ancient Proto-City Reveals the Origin of Home

By Annalee Newitz

The Konya Plain in central Turkey is a vast, elevated plateau covered in small farms and dusty fields, edged by dramatic mountain ranges that cast purple shadows. At night, visitors can drive into the foothills and see distant city lights, shimmering like a mirage. The view here has not changed much over the past 9,000 years—even the illuminated metropolitan skyline would look familiar to a visitor from 7,000 B.C.E. That is because the Konya Plain is one of the cradles of urban life.

Millennia before the rise of Mesopotamian cities to the south, the proto-city Çatalhöyük (pronounced "Chah-tahl-hew-yook") thrived here. Sprawled over 34 acres and home to as many as 8,000 people, it was the metropolis of its day. People lived in this community continuously for almost 2,000 years, before slowly abandoning it in the 5,000s B.C.E. During its heyday, bonfires from the many parties held at Çatalhöyük would have been visible far across the flat grasslands.

Unlike later cities, Çatalhöyük had no great monuments nor any marketplaces. Think of it as a dozen agricultural villages that grew together, forming what some researchers call a "mega site." People entered its thousands of tightly packed, mud-brick homes through ceiling doors, and they navigated sidewalks that wound around the city's rooftops. They planted tiny farm plots around the city. Whether they were fixing up their houses or making clothes, tools, food and art, Çatalhöyük residents spent most of their days between four walls, right next to their bed platforms—or, in warmer months, on their roofs.

This was not exactly what archaeologists expected to find when they first began excavating at Çatalhöyük in the early 1960s. Based on what they knew of other ancient cities, these investigators were primed to discover shrines, markets and priceless loot. Instead they found the remains of home decor, cookware and ritual items associated with domesticity rather than formal churches. The mismatch between expectation and reality flummoxed Çatalhöyük researchers for decades. It took a new kind of archaeologist to figure out what it all meant, piecing together what life was really like when humans were transitioning from a nomadic existence to a settled one as farmers and urbanites with a strong sense of home.

Dido's House

In 2000 archaeologist Ruth Tringham of the University of California, Berkeley, traveled to Çatalhöyük to visit a house that had not seen the light for thousands of years. Inside the structure she discovered the remains of a woman buried under a bed platform. Tringham nicknamed her Dido and returned every summer for the next several years with a team of researchers to excavate Dido's house. The group analyzed everything from the animal figurines and bones found inside to the many layers of plaster paint on its walls.

What they found was a household where everything was made from scratch–including the scratch itself, as it were. It is hard for modern people to imagine the intensity of the labor required to maintain a settled life back in Dido's day. If you wanted to cook dinner, you grew or hunted the food, built your own oven, made cooking tools such as obsidian knives, molded clay pots, then started cooking. People made their own bricks, built their own houses, wove mats for the floors out of reeds and sewed their own clothes (and made the needles, thread and textiles).

Even spirituality seems to have been handcrafted. People buried their loved ones underneath the floors, perhaps as a way to keep them close, and reverently decorated their skulls with plaster and paint. Archaeologists have found similar skulls at other sites dating to the Neolithic–the time spanning 12,000 to 6,500 B.C.E. in the Fertile Crescent–such as Jericho in the West Bank. It appears to have been relatively common at this time to honor the dead by recreating their faces using plaster applied to their skulls. At Çatalhöyük, people sometimes traded these skulls with other families and reburied them at a later time. Researchers often find several skulls buried alongside one body, suggesting that these rituals linked kin to their homes over several generations.

Archaeologists have found elaborate paintings on the interior house walls that were refreshed every year in the same patterns—as if generations of inhabitants wanted to keep the original paintings intact. Some of these patterns are abstract designs of swirls or zigzags, like the ancient equivalent of wallpaper. Others invoke scenes of wild animals and hunters. There are even some wall paintings that appear to shed light on the spiritual underpinnings of the skull ritual: in one house, researchers found a wall painting of headless bodies surrounded by vultures, giving the impression that the birds are bearing people's spirits away.

Animal bones, too, adorn the homes. Nearly every household had its own wall-mounted "bucranium," a plastered bull's skull painted deep red, its sharp horns pointing into the room. People also hid claws and teeth from dangerous animals in the mud brick of their walls in the way people today sometimes put a lucky penny into the foundation of a house.

In the 1960s archaeologists were confounded by finding these obviously symbolic, quasi-religious items mixed in with regular household garbage. One early researcher, James Melaart, thought the entire city must be a giant, mysterious shrine. But "it's only a mystery if you expect it to be something else, something bigger and more complex," Tringham says. Melaart and his colleagues expected to find spiritual objects in grand temples, not in people's kitchens. Tringham always preferred to let the evidence speak for itself, without preconceptions.

Stanford University archaeologist Ian Hodder, who led excavations at Çatalhöyük until 2018, supported Tringham's methods. Traditionally archaeologists had studied artifacts by stealing them from dig sites and bringing them back to museums. Hodder popularized the idea of "contextual archaeology," which suggests that we should understand artifacts not in isolation but by thinking about how they fit into the place where they were discovered. In the case of Çatalhöyük, contextual archaeology gave researchers such as Tringham a framework for interpreting why there were sacred objects in the middle of living rooms. It was because people were fashioning ritual spaces in their own homes.

In contrast to later cities, where separate spaces were built for worship, work and domestic life, Çatalhöyük residents merged them all together under one roof. That is why every house looked like a combination of temple, workshop and bedroom. Hodder believes that these multipurpose houses represent a key stage in the process of human domestication, when many people stopped leading nomadic lives and settled down to farm. At first, houses were just places to sleep and work. But over time, as Hodder puts it, people became "entangled" psychologically with their land–you might say they went from being a bunch of farmers living on Konya Plain to being Çatalites. The city was part of their identities, and they attributed a spiritual meaning to the places where they lived. In the process, houses became homes. In cities built later, there were separate spaces for worship, work and domestic life–but the idea that the city was a home, and not just a resting place, continued to endure.

Instant Soup in the Neolithic

Çatalhöyük shows what everyday life was like at a time when "home" was a radical new idea. Inhabitants had to do many jobs to keep their houses and families intact, but they spent the most time acquiring and making food. We know that they were agriculturalists, tending family farms and flocks of animals on the fertile Konya Plain, which would have afforded them the stable food supply they needed to live year-round in permanent homes. They made a variety of cooking implements, from butcher's knives to soup bowls. And now, thanks to a high-tech analysis of their stew pots, we know what they ate.

"It was like a crime story," says archaeologist Eva Rosenstock with a laugh, as she describes how she and her colleague Jessica

Hendy used forensics methods to extract telltale molecules from ancient food stuck to the inside of cooking vessels. Rosenstock is a research associate at the Einstein Center Chronoi in Berlin, and she has been studying foods and health during the Neolithic for most of her career. She met Hendy a few years ago at a conference, where Hendy was explaining how she had figured out what people ate in the Middle Ages by examining calcium deposits on their tooth enamel. Trapped inside that calcium were traces of lipids and proteins, chemicals found in all living things–including the ones we eat. Hendy could identify medieval foods by cross-referencing the molecular structures of the lipids and proteins on people's dirty teeth with those from known animals and plants.

It was a moment of inspiration for Rosenstock. She had examined a few clay bowl fragments from Çatalhöyük that had a thin calcite layer on the inside, "kind of like limescale in teapots," she explained. She convinced Hendy to examine those ancient dishes for molecules that would reveal Neolithic menu items.

There was a nail-biting period when Hendy started the analysis and her first matches were with exotic aquarium fish and lotus flowers–the result of contamination of the sample with modern molecules. Luckily, further analysis showed that there were much closer molecular matches to other edibles–and these were the real deal. Rosenstock, Hendy and their colleagues discovered traces of peas, wheat, barley, goat, sheep, cattle and even some deer. But the most interesting discovery by far was that all the bowls had held milk at a time before most humans evolved the genetic mutation that allows us to metabolize milk products as adults. Indeed, the dairy remains at Çatalhöyük are among the oldest ever recovered. This does not mean Çatalhöyük diners were getting sick in the way lactose-intolerant people do now. Recent research shows that our gut microbiome–all the microorganisms that live in our intestines–can help us digest milk. The researchers had simply gotten a rare glimpse of the moment when adults began to cook with milk. Over the next several thousand years the mutation that helps people digest dairy into adulthood spread throughout Europe and the Middle East.

Rosenstock believes these milk residues also reveal an ancient laborsaving strategy. Back in the Neolithic, dairy would have been seasonal. Animals gave birth in the spring, and their milk would have dried up by winter. To enjoy milk year-round, communities all across the world invented cheese and other fermented dairy foods that could keep for a long time. In Turkey and nearby regions, people prepare a dried sour milk dish known variously as *qurut* or *kashk*. Sometimes it is molded into balls and sometimes powdered; for added flavor, the milk can be fermented with ground grains, too. People at Çatalhöyük might have been making a similar dish. "You get this super storable thing that won't go rancid for years," Rosenstock says. "You put it in hot water, and it's like instant soup!" Perfect for a hot meal at home on a cold winter day, when nobody wants to go outside to farm or hunt.

The Clay Ball Mystery

Crafters at Çatalhöyük had other laborsaving tricks as well. Roughly 8,500 years ago, centuries after the city's founding, fired pottery was invented–and it was as revolutionary for Neolithic cooks as microwaves were for impatient, hungry people in the 1970s. Before the rise of ceramics, cooking was a labor-intensive process. University of Massachusetts Amherst anthropologist Sonya Atalay found evidence that stews were made in watertight woven baskets. You put your water and ingredients into the basket and heated it with large stones or clay balls heated in the fire. When the balls cooled, you took them out and replaced them with hot ones. It was no doubt a tiresome process, especially after a long day of gathering food and water.

Atalay's portrait of preceramic kitchen life came from two sources of evidence. First, there are a few modern people who still cook with heated stones because it is part of their cultural traditions. And second, the settlement of Çatalhöyük is simply bursting with piles of large clay balls, about the size of grapefruits, that are covered in scorch marks from fires. Some houses have hundreds of them, scattered in and around hearths. To Atalay, it seemed obvious that these clay balls were cooking stones.

After the rise of ceramics at Çatalhöyük, people mostly stopped making large clay balls and woven cooking baskets. Because ceramic pots are heat-resistant, they could be put on stands over the fire to simmer stews all day. It must have felt incredibly luxurious to cook without constantly juggling hot clay balls.

There is just one problem with this story. When scientists analyzed these clay balls for lipids and proteins akin to the ones found on Rosenstock's bowls, they found nothing. It would appear the balls were heated and clearly used in the kitchen, but they were not ever submerged in food. So what were they for?

Lucy Bennison-Chapman, an archaeology researcher at Leiden University in the Netherlands, spent years analyzing the balls and made some surprising discoveries. Although she does not completely rule out their use in stews, she thinks that is extremely unlikely–they were simply too big and would have shed bits of clay and dirt into the food. She also dismisses the possibility that they were weapons. "They're different from sling missiles," she says. "They're smaller and generally a different shape."

Instead she thinks the large balls were heaters. In some cases, they were used to line the bottoms of ovens to hold warmth. They could also have been the Stone Age equivalent of heating trays–people might have pulled the balls from the fire, covered them in reed mats and placed food on top. There is yet another possibility, which will be familiar to anyone who has read a Charles Dickens novel where someone puts heated bricks in their bed at night. "On the Konya Plain, it gets really cold in winter. You could heat them and use them as a body warmer. Or you could wrap them in linen and put them in your bedding," Bennison-Chapman explains. "People worked on rooftops and in the fields, so you could place heated balls in your pockets while you were outside. This would explain why they were reheated and reused so often."

Making these multifunctional balls was incredibly time-consuming. "They would have spent a long time going over them with their hands, smoothing them," Bennison-Chapman says. "They're covered in fingerprints." Perhaps because it took so long to make them, the balls were used over and over, reheated in the fire until they were cracked. Most balls found at Çatalhöyük have been reduced to fragments. Some were recycled and turned into packing material in mud bricks or were placed between walls, perhaps for insulation.

Clay balls also figure importantly at Çatalhöyük for another reason. In addition to the big heaters, residents made miniature clay balls, which were occasionally decorated with dots and other patterns. These mini balls, or tokens, are the earliest examples at Çatalhöyük of "counting pieces," named by archaeologists who believed they were for simple record keeping or tallying up resources. Bennison-Chapman cautions, however, that tokens were not purpose-built for counting–they probably served as gaming pieces, weights, ritual objects and even just decoration. Still, the tokens show that domestic life was not simply focused on cooking and staying cozy. Crafting objects at Çatalhöyük would eventually lead to counting and written language.

No Place Like Home

The Neolithic was a period of rapid change for humanity, especially when it came to defining what it meant to be at home. Before about 12,000 years ago, very few people lived in agricultural settlements year-round–most were nomadic or seminomadic, living in small groups as hunter-gatherers who moved from site to site according to seasonal changes in food availability. So when people finally did begin to build permanent houses and form larger settlements, they had to figure out new ways of living in one place, cheek by jowl with their neighbors.

Mostly they did it by building those homes together–sharing the backbreaking labor but also the joys of community. John S. Allen, an anthropology researcher at Indiana University Bloomington, is author of the 2015 book *Home: How Habitat Made Us Human*.

"A home is a space you have an emotional attachment to, through habitual use," he says. Humans create homes by forming an association between their community and a specific place, he adds. This might be one reason graves at Çatalhöyük lay just below the floors of homes. "A burial signifies a special place for family and friends," Allen suggests, underscoring the idea of a home as an emotional space as well as a practical one.

When Rosenstock described all the foods that people ate at Çatalhöyük, one topic came up again and again: her intense conviction that sooner or later she and her colleagues will find evidence for beer. Partly that is because archaeologists have found evidence of beer production in other Neolithic cultures around the world. But it is also because there is so much evidence for merrymaking at Çatalhöyük. "They have massive amounts of pottery–they're creating and discarding it like crazy. You can't help but think they were eating and smashing the pots," she says. They also threw away bones that still had meat on them, as if they were feasting and drinking.

Building a city is not all about work. It's about parties, too. Perhaps, at the dawn of city life, working and partying were two sides of the same coin: they were the tissues that knit us together in a single place we came to know as home.

About the Author

Annalee Newitz is a science journalist and author based in Irvine, Calif. Their latest book is Four Lost Cities: A Secret History of the Urban Age *(W. W. Norton, 2021).*

Section 4: You Are What You Eat

Case for (Very) Early Cooking Heats Up

By Kate Wong

With our supersized brains and shrunken teeth and guts, we humans are bizarre primates. Richard Wrangham of Harvard University has long argued that these and other peculiar traits of our kind arose as humans turned to cooking to improve food quality—making it softer and easier to digest and thus a richer source of energy. Humans, unlike any other animal, cannot survive on raw food in the wild, he observes. "We need to have our food cooked."

Based on the anatomy of our fossil forebears, Wrangham thinks that *Homo erectus* had mastered cooking with fire by 1.8 million years ago. Critics have countered that he lacks evidence to support the claim that cooking enhances digestibility and that the oldest known traces of fire are nowhere near as old as his hypothesis predicts. New findings, Wrangham says, lend support to his ideas.

Scientific American: How did you come up with the cooking hypothesis?

Wrangham: I think of two strands. One is that I was trying to figure out what was responsible for the evolution of the human body form, and I was sensitive to the fact that humans everywhere use fire. I started thinking about how long ago you would have to go back before humans did not use fire. And that suggested to me the hypothesis that they always used it because they would not have survived without it. Humans as a genus [*Homo*] are committed to sleeping on the ground. I do not want to sleep on the ground in Africa without fire to keep the wild animals at bay.

The other strand is that I've studied chimpanzees and their feeding behavior for many years. I've eaten everything that I can get ahold of that chimpanzees eat. And I have been very much aware of the deeply unsatisfying nature of those foods because they are often quite fibrous, relatively dry, and contain little sugar, and they are often strong-tasting—in other words, really nasty. So here we are, two very closely related species with completely different dietary habits. It was an obvious hypothesis that cooking does something special for the food we find in nature. But I was astonished to discover that there was no systematic evidence showing what cooking does to the net energetic gain that we get from our foods.

For the past 14 years I've been focused on that question because to make a satisfactory claim about humans being adapted to cooked food, we have to produce some real evidence about what cooking does to food. Experiments conducted by Rachel N. Carmody of Harvard University have now given us the evidence: if we cook, we get more energy from our food.

Q: Other researchers hold that increased access to meat allowed the teeth and gut to shrink. Why do you think cooking better explains these changes?

A: It's quite clear that humans began eating meat from large animals by 2.5 million years ago and have left a steady record of cut marks on bones since then. The cooking hypothesis does not deny the importance of meat eating. But there is a core difficulty with attributing changes in digestive anatomy to this shift.

Selection pressure on digestive anatomy is strongest when food is scarce. Under such conditions, animals have very little fat on them, and fat-poor meat is a very poor food because if you have more than about 30 percent protein in your diet, then your ability to get rid of ammonia fast enough is overwhelmed. Nowadays in surveys of hunters and gatherers, what you find is that during periods of food scarcity, there is always a substantial inclusion of plants. Very often it's tubers. To eat those raw, you would have to have the digestive apparatus to handle tough, fibrous, low-carbohydrate plant foods—that is, large teeth and a big gut.

Q: So your idea is that by cooking those plant foods, our ancestors could evolve a smaller gut and teeth—and avoid overdosing

on lean meat. Let's turn now to what happened when food was not so scarce and animals were good to eat. You have argued that cooking may have helped early humans eat more meat by freeing them up to hunt. What is your logic?

A: A primate the size of an early human would be expected to spend about half of its day chewing, as chimpanzees do. Modern humans spend less than an hour a day, whether you're American or living in various subsistence societies around the world. So you've got four or five hours a day freed by the fact that you're eating relatively soft food. In hunter-gatherer life, men tend to spend this time hunting.

That observation raises the question of how much hunting was possible until our ancestors were able to reduce the amount of time they chewed. Chimpanzees like to eat meat, but their average hunt is just 20 minutes, after which they go back to eating fruit. Hunting is risky. If you fail, then you need to be able to eat your ordinary food. If you hunt too long without success, you won't have enough time to process your usual, lower-quality fare. It seems to me that it was only after cooking enabled individuals to save time on chewing that they could increase the amount of time spent on an activity that, for all its potential benefits, might not yield any food.

Q: You have also suggested that cooking allowed the brain to expand. How would cooking do that?

A: With regard to the brain, fossils indicate a fairly steady increase in cranial capacity, starting shortly before 2 million years ago. There are lots of ideas about why selection favored larger brains, but the question of how our ancestors could afford them has been a puzzle. The problem is that brains use a disproportionate amount of energy and can never be turned off.

I have extended the idea put forward by Leslie C. Aiello, now at the Wenner-Gren Foundation in New York City, and Peter Wheeler of Liverpool John Moores University in England that after cooking became obligatory, the increase in food quality contributed to reduced gut size. Their newly small guts were energetically cheaper, allowing calories to be diverted to the brain.

In 2012 Karina Fonseca-Azevedo and Suzana Herculano-Houzel of the Federal University of Rio de Janeiro added a new wrinkle. Their calculations showed that on a raw diet, the number of calories needed to support a human-sized brain would require too many hours eating every day. They argued that cooking allowed our ancestors the extra energy needed to support more neurons, allowing the increase in brain size.

Q: Cooking is not the only way to make food easier to digest. How does it compare with other methods?

A: Simply reducing the size of food particles and the structural integrity of food–through pounding, for example–makes it easier to digest. Carmody did a study that looked at tubers and meat as representative types of food that hunter-gatherers eat and asked how well mice fared when eating each of these foods, either raw versus cooked or whole versus pounded. She very carefully controlled the amount of food that the mice received, along with the amount of energy they expended moving around, and assessed their net energetic gain through looking at body-mass changes. She found that pounding had relatively little effect, whereas cooking led to significant increases in body weight whether the food was tubers or meat.

This is incredibly exciting because, amazingly, this is the first study that has ever been done to show that animals get more net energy out of their food when it is cooked than when it's raw. Second, it showed that even if pounding has some positive effects on energy gain, cooking has much bigger effects. [*Editors' note: Wrangham was a co-author on the study, published in 2011.*]

Q: Is there any genetic evidence to support the cooking hypothesis?

A: There is essentially nothing published yet. But we're very aware that a really interesting question is going to be whether or not we can detect, in the human genome, evidence of selection for genes related to utilizing cooked food. They might be concerned with metabolism. They might be concerned with the immune system. They might be concerned somehow with responses to Maillard compounds, which are somewhat dangerous compounds produced by cooking. This is going to be a very exciting area in the future.

Q: A central objection to the cooking hypothesis has been that there is no archaeological evidence of controlled fire as far back as the hypothesis predicts. Currently the oldest traces come from 1-million-year-old deposits in Wonderwerk Cave in South Africa. But you have recently identified an independent line of evidence that humans tamed fire earlier than the archaeological record suggests. How does that work support your thinking?

A: Chimpanzees love honey, yet they eat very little of it because they get chased away by bees. African hunters and gatherers, in contrast, eat somewhere between 100 and 1,000 times as much honey as chimpanzees do because they use fire. Smoke interferes with the olfactory system of the bees, and under those conditions, the bees do not attack. The question is: How long have humans been using smoke to get honey? That's where the honeyguide comes in. The greater honeyguide is an African species of bird that is adapted to guiding humans to honey. The bird is attracted to human activity–sounds of chopping, whistling, shouting, banging and, nowadays, motor vehicles. On finding people, the bird starts fluttering in front of them and then leads them off with a special call and waits for them to follow. Honeyguides can lead humans a kilometer or more to a tree that has honey in it. The human then uses smoke to disarm the bees and opens the hive up with an ax to extract the honey inside. The bird gains access to the hive's wax, which it eats.

It used to be thought that the bird's guiding behavior [which is innate, not learned] originated in partnership with the honey badger and that humans moved in on this arrangement later. But in the past 30 years it has become very clear that honey badgers are rarely, if ever, led to honey by honeyguides. If there's no living species other than humans that has this symbiotic relationship with the bird, could there have been some extinct species of something that favored the honeyguide showing this behavior? Well, obviously, the most reasonable candidates are the extinct ancestors of humans. The argument points very strongly to our ancestors having used fire long enough for natural selection to enable this relationship to develop.

Claire Spottiswoode of the University of Cambridge discovered that there are two kinds of greater honeyguide females: those that lay their eggs in ground nests and those that lay in tree nests. Then she found that the two types of behavior are associated with different lineages of mitochondrial DNA [DNA that is found in the energy-producing components of cells and passed down from mother to offspring]. Based on a fairly conservative assessment of the rate of mutation, Spottiswoode and her colleagues determined that the two lineages had been separated for about 3 million years, [providing a minimum estimate for the age of the greater honeyguide species]. That doesn't necessarily mean that the guiding habit, which depends on humans using fire, is that old–it could be more recent–but at least it tells you that the species is old enough to allow for much evolutionary change.

Q: If cooking was a driving force in human evolution, does this conclusion have implications for how people should eat today?

A: It does remind us that eating raw food is a very different proposition from eating cooked food. Because we don't think about the consequences of processing our food, we are getting a misunderstanding of the net energy gain from eating. One of the ways in which this can be quite serious is if people who are dedicated to a raw-food diet don't understand the consequences for their children. If you just say, "Well, animals eat their food raw, and humans are animals, then it should be fine for us to eat our food raw," and you bring your children up this way, you're putting them at very severe risk. We are a different species from every other. It's fine to eat raw food if you want to lose weight. But if you want to gain weight, as with a child or an adult who's too thin, then you don't want to eat a raw diet.

Referenced

Energetic Consequences of Thermal and Nonthermal Food Processing. Rachel N. Carmody et al. in *Proceedings of the National Academy of Sciences USA*, Vol. 108, No. 48, pages 19199–19203; November 29, 2011.

Honey and Fire in Human Evolution. Richard Wrangham in *Casting the Net Wide: Papers in Honor of Glynn Isaac and His Approach to Human Origins Research*. Edited by Jeanne Sept and David Pilbeam. Oxbow Books, 2012.

Metabolic Constraint Imposes Tradeoff between Body Size and Number of Brain Neurons in Human Evolution. Karina Fonseca-Azevedo and Suzana Herculano-Houzel in *Proceedings of the National Academy of Sciences USA*, Vol. 109, No. 45, pages 18,571–18,576; November 6, 2012.

About the Author

Kate Wong is a senior editor at Scientific American.

Human Evolution Led to an Extreme Thirst for Water

By Asher Y. Rosinger

We trekked through the Bolivian Amazon, drenched in sweat. Draped head to toe in bug repellent gear, we stayed just ahead of the clouds of mosquitoes as we sidestepped roots, vines and giant ants. My local research assistant Dino Nate, my partner Kelly Rosinger and I were following Julio, one of my Tsimane' friends and our guide on this day. Tsimane' are a group of forager-horticulturalists who live in this hot, humid region. Just behind us, Julio's three-year-old son floated happily through the jungle, unfazed by the heat and insects despite his lack of protective clothing, putting my perspiration-soaked efforts to shame.

We stopped in front of what looked like a small tree but turned out to be a large vine. Julio told us Tsimane' use it when they are in the old-growth forest and need water. He began whacking at the vine from all sides with his machete, sending chips of bark flying with each stroke. Within two minutes he had cut off a meter-long section. Water started to pour out of it. He held it over his mouth, drinking from it for a few seconds to quench his thirst, then offered it to me. I put my water bottle under the vine and collected a cup. It tasted pretty good: light, a little chalky, almost carbonated.

As part of my field research, I was asking Julio and other Tsimane' people how they obtain the drinking water they need in different places–in their homes, in the fields, on the river or in the forest. He told me only two types of vines are used for water; the rest don't work or make you sick. But when he pointed to those other vines, I could hardly tell a difference. The vines are a hidden source of water. Julio's observations raise a fundamental question of human adaptation: How did our evolutionary history shape the strategies we use to meet our water needs, particularly in environments without ready access to clean water?

Here in the forest we were in a relatively water-rich environment, but as we moved away from streams, Julio still knew exactly where and how to get water. Humans are not alone in keeping close track of natural water sources—many animals make mental maps of their surroundings to remember where important resources are found, and some even alter their environments for water. But we are unique in taking much more extreme measures.

Throughout history people have drastically engineered their environments to ensure access to water. Take the historic Roman city of Caesarea in modern-day Israel. Back when it was built, more than 2,000 years ago, the region did not have enough naturally occurring freshwater to sustain a city. Because of its geographic importance to their colonial rule, the Romans, through extractive slave labor, built a series of aqueducts to transport water from springs as far as 16 kilometers away. This arrangement provided up to 50,000 people with approximately 145 liters of water per capita a day.

Today cities use vast distribution networks to provide potable water to people, which has led to remarkable improvements in public health. When we have plenty of water, we forget how critical it truly is. But when water is precious, it is all we think about. All it takes is news of a shutoff or contamination event for worries about water insecurity to take hold.

Without enough water, our physical and cognitive functions decline. Without any, we die within a matter of days. In this way, humans are more dependent on water than many other mammals are. Recent research has illuminated the origins of our water needs—and how we adapted to quench that thirst. It turns out that much as food has shaped human evolution, so, too, has water.

Breaking a Sweat

To understand how water has influenced the course of human evolution, we need to page back to a pivotal chapter of our prehistory. Between around 3 million and 2 million years ago, the climate in Africa, where hominins (members of the human family) first evolved, became drier. During this interval, the early hominin genus *Australopithecus* gave way to our own genus, *Homo*. In the course of this transition, body proportions changed: whereas australopithecines were short and stocky, *Homo* had a taller, slimmer build with more surface area. These changes reduced our ancestors' exposure to solar radiation while allowing for greater exposure to wind, which increased their ability to dissipate heat, making them more water-efficient.

Other key adaptations accompanied this shift in body plan. As climate change replaced forests with grasslands, and early hominins became more proficient at traveling on two legs in open environments, they lost their body hair and developed more sweat glands. These adaptations increased our ancestors' ability to unload excess heat and thus maintain a safe body temperature while moving, as work by Nina Jablonski of Pennsylvania State University and Peter Wheeler of Liverpool John Moores University in England has shown.

Sweat glands are a crucial part of our story. Mammals have three types of sweat glands: apocrine, sebaceous and eccrine. The eccrine glands mobilize the water and electrolytes inside cells to produce sweat. Humans have more eccrine sweat glands than any other primate. A recent study by Daniel Aldea of the University of Pennsylvania and his colleagues found that repeated mutations of a gene called *Engrailed 1* may have led to this abundance of eccrine sweat glands. In relatively dry environments akin to the ones early hominins evolved in, the evaporation of sweat cools the skin and blood vessels, which, in turn, cools the body's core.

Armed with this powerful cooling system, early humans could afford to be more active than other primates. In fact, some researchers think that persistence hunting–running an animal down until it overheats–may have been an important foraging strategy for our ancestors, one they could not have pursued if they did not have a means to avoid overheating.

This enhanced sweating ability has a downside, however: it elevates our risk of dehydration. Martin Hora of Charles University in Prague and his collaborators recently demonstrated that *Homo erectus* would have been able to persistence hunt for approximately five hours in the hot savanna before losing 10 percent of its body mass. In humans, 10 percent body mass loss from dehydration is generally the cutoff before serious risk of physiological and cognitive problems or even death occurs. Beyond that point, drinking becomes difficult, and intravenous fluids are needed for rehydration.

Our vulnerability to dehydration means that we are more reliant on external sources of water than our primate cousins and far more than desert-adapted animals such as sheep, camels and goats, which can lose 20 to 40 percent of their body water without risking death. These animals have an extra compartment in the gut called the forestomach that can store water as an internal buffer against dehydration.

In fact, desert-dwelling mammals have a range of adaptations to water scarcity. Some of these traits have to do with the functioning of the kidneys, which maintain the body's water and salt balance. Mammals vary in the size and shape of their kidneys and thus the extent to which they can concentrate urine and thereby conserve body water. The desert pocket mouse, for example, can live without water for months, in part because of the extreme extent to which its kidneys can concentrate urine. Humans can do this to a degree. When we lose copious amounts of water from sweating, a complex network of hormones and neural circuitry directs our kidneys to conserve water by concentrating urine. But our limited ability to do so means we cannot go without freshwater for nearly so long as the pocket mouse.

Neither can we preload our bodies with water. The desert camel can drink and store enough water to draw on for weeks. But if humans drink too much fluid, our urine output quickly increases. Our gut size and the rate at which our stomach empties limit how fast we can rehydrate. Worse, if we drink too much water too fast, we can throw off our electrolyte balance and develop hyponatremia—abnormally low levels of sodium in the blood—which is just as deadly if not more so than dehydration.

Even under favorable conditions, with food and water readily available, people generally do not recover all of their water losses from heavy exercise for at least 24 hours. And so we must be careful to strike a balance in how we lose and replenish the water in our bodies.

Quenching Our Thirst

There was a reason I was asking Julio about "hidden" sources of water, such as vines, that Tsimane' consumed. One evening after dinner a few weeks into my first bout of fieldwork in Bolivia in 2009, the combination of thirst and hunger led me to devour a large papaya. The juices ran down my chin as I ate the ripe fruit. I didn't think much of it at the moment, but soon after I got into my mosquito net for the night, my error revealed itself.

In the Bolivian Amazon, the humidity reaches up to 100 percent at night. Every evening before going to bed I stripped down to my boxers, then rolled my clothes up tightly and put them into large resealable plastic bags so they wouldn't be soaked the next morning. After about an hour of lying in my mosquito net praying for a gust of wind to cool me off, a dreaded sensation set in: I needed to urinate. Knowing the amount of work it would take to get dressed, relieve myself, and then refold and stow my clothes, I cursed my decision to eat the papaya. And I had to repeat the process again later that night. I started thinking about how much water was in that fruit–the equivalent of three cups, it turns out. No wonder I had to pee.

Our dietary flexibility is perhaps our best defense against dehydration. As I learned the hard way on that sweltering night, the amount of water present in food contributes to total water intake. In the U.S., around 20 percent of the water people ingest comes from food, yet my work among Tsimane' found that foods, including fruits, contribute up to 50 percent of their total water intake. Adults in Japan, who typically drink less water than adults in the U.S., also get around half their water from the foods they eat. Other populations employ different dietary strategies to meet their water needs. Daasanach pastoralists in northern Kenya consume a great deal of milk, which is 87 percent water. They also chew on water-laden roots.

Chimpanzees, our closest living primate relatives, also exhibit dietary and behavioral adaptations to obtaining water. They lick wet rocks and use leaves as sponges to collect water. Primatologist Jill Pruetz of Texas State University has found that in very hot environments, such as the savannas at Fongoli in Senegal, chimps seek shelter in cool caves and forage at night rather than during the day to minimize heat stress and conserve body water. But overall nonhuman primates get most of their water from fruits, leaves and other foods.

Humans have evolved to use less water than chimps and other apes, despite our greater sweating ability, as new research by Herman Pontzer of Duke University and his colleagues has shown. Yet our greater reliance on plain water as opposed to water from food means that we must work hard to stay hydrated. Exactly how much water is healthy differs between populations and even from person to person, however. Currently there are two different recommendations for water intake, which includes water from food. The first, from the U.S. National Academy of Medicine, recommends 3.7 liters of water a day for men and 2.7 liters for women, while advising pregnant and lactating women to increase their intake by 300 and 700 milliliters, respectively. The second, from the European Food Safety Authority, recommends 2.5 and 2.0 liters a day for men and women, respectively, with the same increases for pregnant and lactating women. Men need more water than women do because their bodies are larger and have more muscle on average.

These are not hard-and-fast recommendations. They were calculated from population averages based on surveys and studies of people in specific regions. They are intended to fulfill the majority of water needs for moderately active, healthy people living in temperate and often climate-controlled environments. Some people may need more or less water depending on factors that include life habits, climate, activity level and age.

In fact, water intake varies widely even in relatively water-secure locations such as the U.S. Most men consume between 1.2 and 6.3 liters on a given day and women between 1.0 and 5.1 liters. Throughout human evolution our ancestors' water intake probably also varied substantially based on activity level, temperature, and exposure to wind and solar radiation, along with body size and water availability.

Yet it is also the case that two people of similar age and physical condition living in the same environment can consume drastically different amounts of water and both be healthy, at least in the short term. Such variation may relate to early life experiences. Humans undergo a sensitive period during fetal development that influences many physiological functions, among them how our bodies balance water. We receive cues about our nutritional environment while in the womb and during nursing. This information may shape the offspring's water needs.

Experimental studies have demonstrated that water restriction among pregnant rats and sheep leads to critical changes in how their offspring detect bodily dehydration. Offspring born to such water-deprived mothers will be more dehydrated (that is, their urine and blood will be more concentrated) than offspring born to nondeprived mothers before they become thirsty and seek out water. These findings indicate that the dehydration-sensitivity set point is established in the womb.

Thus, the hydration cues received during development may determine when people perceive thirst, as well as how much water they drink later in life. In a sense, these early experiences prepare offspring for the amount of water present in their environment. If a pregnant woman is dealing with a water-scarce environment and is chronically dehydrated, it may lead to her child consistently drinking less water later in life—a trait that is adaptive in places where water is hard to come by. Much more work is needed to test this theory, however.

Keeping it Clean

Although early life experiences may determine how much water we drink without our being aware of it, locating safe sources of water is something we actively learn to do. In contrast to my accidental discovery of the hydrating effects of the papaya, Tsimane' deliberately seek out water-rich foods. In an environment without clean water, eating instead of drinking more water may protect against exposures to pathogens. Indeed, my study found that those Tsimane' who consumed more of their water from foods and fruit, such as papayas, were less likely to experience diarrhea.

Many societies have developed dietary traditions that incorporate low-alcohol, fermented beverages, which can be essential sources of hydration because fermentation kills bacteria. (Beverages containing higher percentages of alcohol, on the other hand, increase urine production and thereby deplete the body's water stores.) Like other Amazonian populations, Tsimane' drink a fermented beverage called chicha that is made from yuca or cassava. For Tsimane' men, consuming fermented chicha was associated with lower odds of becoming dehydrated.

Getting enough water is one of humanity's oldest and most pressing challenges. Perhaps it is not surprising, then, that we map the locations of water sources in our minds, whether it is a highway rest stop, desert spring or jungle plant. As I watched Julio cut the vine down, his son was also watching, learning where this critical water source was. I glimpsed how this process plays out across generations. In so doing, I realized that being covered in sweat and finding ways to replace that lost water is a big part of what makes us human.

About the Author

Asher Y. Rosinger is a human biologist at Pennsylvania State University. He studies human variation in water intake and how this relates to environmental resources and health and disease risk.

Our 14,400-Year-Old Relationship with Bread

By Krystal D'Costa

Indians have roti, naan, paratha, and daal puri. Armenians have lavash. Ethiopians have injera. The French have the boule, brioche, and baguette. The British have scones. And the Polish have challah. These are but a few of the different types of breads that are enjoyed around the world. Despite its widespread existence, however, bread is regarded by many as a "bad" food, and many willingly avoid it (without health concerns, like gluten intolerance, as a driving factor). And yet according to a recent study our relationship with bread may date back to at least 14,400 years ago. It may be even older but that's just the point where we have proof bread existed. Why is this significant? It changes our understanding of how our human ancestors may have eaten and potentially how they may have interacted with their environment. And it challenges what we think we know about how to eat.

In the Black Desert region of northeast Jordan, a group of hunter-gatherers set up camp somewhere between 14.5–11.6 thousand years ago. Well, it may have been a little more than a camp as the findings report that the site–known as Shubayqa 1–includes two well-preserved superimposed *buildings*. These were semi-subterranean structures with a flagstone path constructed from local basalt. The older building is referred to as Structure 1 and it is within Structure 1 where two fireplaces were built sequentially that our story unfolds. The inhabitants of the site neglected to clean the older fireplace after its last use; this fireplace was covered by a deposit of about .5 meter that blanketed the building. Subsequent occupants to Shubayqa 1 built another fireplace over the original. They, too, left the fireplace intact following their last use. It is from these structures that bread-like materials and charred plant remains were recovered. Of the plants the most common sample was of club-rush tubers, which is notable because this plant lends itself to flour production in order to be consumed.

Archaeologists recovered twenty-two "bread-like" remains from the older fireplace, and two from the more recent fireplace. Anyone who has had some experience with bread knows that while it may be calorically filling, it's not exactly likely to last through the ages. So how do we know these finds are prehistoric breads? There are criteria for identifying flat bread, dough, and porridge-like materials in the archaeological record. For bread this means measuring the pores or voids that are created as gas cells expand during cooking. Based on this understanding the remains recovered from Shubayqa 1 are likely an unleavened flat bread product: the voids were about 0.15mm in size and covered about 16% of the samples. These findings were consistent with other "flat breads" recovered from Neolithic and Roman sites in Europe and Turkey.

But if that doesn't convince you, let's take a look at the predominant plant material recovered from the fireplace. Scientists recovered over 65,000 non-woody plan macroremains belonging to at least 95 taxa. While the club-rush tubers were most common, other plants included small seeded legumes, wild wheat, barley, and oat. Ethnobotanical evidence, as well as experiential recreations, suggest that club-rush tubers are better when processed instead of just boiling or steaming. Scientists report that pure club-rush tuber bread is brittle and crumbly, but the addition of wheat flour will create a moldable dough that can be cooked in tandoor-type ovens easily (which is essentially what these fireplaces were). Club-rush tubers were being used in this way in late-Neolithic sites in Turkey and The Netherlands. Additionally 46% of the wild wheat and barley grains recovered at the site showed a bulging pattern on broken edges, which is caused by grinding grains before charring–and also linked to flour making.

We know that bread is a part of our culinary history. It has been found in Neolithic sites throughout Europe and southwest Asia. The prior oldest sample is from Anatolia, Turkey and dates to 9,500 years ago. Everything that has been previously found dates firmly within the agricultural revolution. And that is logical. Making bread is work, after all: you have to cultivate, harvest, dehusk, and grind the cereal grains, and then knead and bake the dough which necessitates the building of a fireplace or oven. This requires time and commitment. But that doesn't mean it was impossible prior to the rise of agriculture.

The inhabitants of Shubayqa 1 weren't pastoral. The remains recovered from Jordan are older and also are tied to a different period in our evolutionary history. Shubayqa 1 is linked to the Natufian culture which is a transitionary period leading to the onset of the Neolithic. The direct descendants of Natufian are believed to be the ones who established agriculture and set us on the course to our present day, but the Natifuan lived semi-sedentary lifestyles. They built camps like those found at Shubayqa 1 but moved about the landscape in accordance with a rhythm that made sense to them. And wheat and barley occurred naturally in southwest Asia, so some populations were already familiar with these grains. Given that the remains recovered are tied to the last uses of the fireplaces in the settlement, it is possible that the residents were making bread to create a portable food item; light, long-lasting, and high in calories, bread would have been ideal for a group on-the-go. Alternatively, given the work required to produce bread, it's possible that this was a festival food, something that would have been eaten on a special occasion.

In either case, bread certainly wouldn't have achieved everyday status until the advent of agriculture. And these finds tell us that these hunter-gatherers were interacting with their spaces differently than the lack of evidence suggested. Hunter-gatherer diets are often discussed in terms of animals and seafoods because these are the remains that have largely been recovered at the sites they occupied. Plant material isn't preserved as well within the fossil record, and we are only just beginning to understand how to analyze what we do find. The remains from Jordan show us that these inhabitants of Subayqa 1 were processing plants and making plant-based foods. And this may have an impact on our present-day dietary pursuits.

In America, at the moment, carbohydrates top the list of bad-for-you-foods and many people are avoiding bread, rice and other related items. The problem is that we actually need carbohydrates, but we often don't make the distinction between simple and complex carbs and everything gets lumped into the bad-for-you label.

The labeling of bread and other carbohydrate friendly foods as "bad" has led to the rise of specialized diets like the Paleo diet, which is meant to mimic the foods our hunter-gatherer ancestors ate 2.6 million years ago until they settled into an agrarian lifestyle. The argument for following a Paleo diet is fueled by the belief that we haven't genetically adapted to eating farmed and processed foods. The Paleo diet maintains we should predominantly eat lean meats and fish, and not include dairy, beans or cereal grains–foods that we believed our hunter-gatherer ancestors did not eat.

But we're learning that our understanding of our ancestor's diets is only as good as what we can find in the archaeological record. The rise of agriculture was not our dietary undoing, although it certainly wrought changes in our lifestyles which undoubtedly impacted our health. Cooking foods gave early humans more energy to devote to brain growth and more calories, so they could gain weight. Modern humans are victims of this success: we have gotten so good at processing and consuming foods that we're getting more calories than we actually can burn in a day. Our relationship with food and food production isn't a static thing. Our understanding didn't peak 15,000 years ago. This relationship is a dynamic one that will continue to unfold as more of our evolutionary history is revealed.

Unless there is a medical reason to avoid carbohydrates or gluten, our complicated relationship with bread may only be complicated because we make it so. And it will remain that way until we're willing to examine in depth what and how we eat.

Referenced

Amaia Arranz-Otaegui, Lara Gonzalez Carretero, Monica N. Ramsey, Dorian Q. Fuller, Tobias Richter. Archaeobotanical evidence reveals the origins of bread 14,400 years ago in northeastern Jordan. *Proceedings of the National Academy of Sciences*, 2018; 201801071 DOI: 10.1073/pnas.1801071115

About the Author

Krystal D'Costa is an anthropologist working in digital media in New York City.

GLOSSARY

anthropology The study of human races, origins, societies, and cultures.

archaeology The study of material remains (such as tools, pottery, jewelry, stone walls, and monuments) of past human life and activities.

archaic Of or relating to ancient times.

Australopithecus Extinct early hominids from southern and eastern Africa.

bipedalism The condition of having two feet or of using only two feet for movement.

genome The genetic material of an organism.

hominid A family of bipedal primate mammals that includes recent humans together with extinct related forms.

hominin A hominid group that includes recent humans together with extinct related forms.

linguistics The study of language and of the way languages work.

megafauna Animals (such as bears, bison, or mammoths) of particularly large size.

Neandertal A hominid known from skeletal remains in Europe, northern Africa, and western Asia that lived from about 30,000 to 200,000 years ago.

paleontology The science that deals with the fossils of animals and plants that lived very long ago.

Pleistocene A period of time between 2 million and 10,000 years ago, characterized by widespread glacial ice and the advent of modern humans.

FURTHER INFORMATION

"New Study: Evolution of Uniquely Human DNA Was a Delicate Balancing Act," *SciTechDaily*, February 27, 2023, https://scitechdaily.com/new-study-evolution-of-uniquely-human-dna-was-a-delicate-balancing-act/.

Clement, Alice. "We can still see these 5 traces of ancestor species in all human bodies today," *The Conversation*, January 22, 2023, https://theconversation.com/we-can-still-see-these-5-traces-of-ancestor-species-in-all-human-bodies-today-197011.

Jablonski, Nina G. "The Naked Truth: Why Humans Have No Fur," *Scientific American*, October 1, 2013, https://www.scientificamerican.com/article/the-naked-truth-why-humans-have-no-fur1/.

Klinghoffer, David. "New Nobel Laureate, Svante Pääbo, on the 'Politics' of Paleontology and Human Origins," *Evolution News*, October 3, 2022, https://evolutionnews.org/2022/10/new-nobel-laureate-svante-paabo-on-the-politics-of-paleontology-and-humans-origins/.

Marean, Curtis W. "How *Homo sapiens* Became the Ultimate Invasive Species," *Scientific American*, August 1, 2015, https://www.scientificamerican.com/article/how-homo-sapiens-became-the-ultimate-invasive-species/.

Marshall, Michael. "Early hominin Paranthropus may have used sophisticated stone tools," *NewScientist*, February 9, 2023, https://www.newscientist.com/article/2358821-early-hominin-paranthropus-may-have-used-sophisticated-stone-tools/.

Taub, Ben. "Neanderthals, Denisovans, And Modern Humans Might Have Intermingled In Iran," *IFLScience*, February 27, 2023, https://www.iflscience.com/neanderthals-denisovans-and-modern-humans-might-have-intermingled-in-iran-67704.

CITATIONS

1.1 Why Is Homo sapiens the Sole Surviving Member of the Human Family? by Kate Wong (September 1, 2018); 1.2 Losing Key DNA Made Us Modern Humans by Philip L. Reno (May 1, 2017); 1.3 Ancient Girl Had Denisovan and Neandertal Parents by Krystal D'Costa (September 6, 2018); 1.4 The Fossil That Rewrote Human Prehistory by Jason Heaton, Travis Rayne Pickering, and Dominic Stratford (September 19, 2016); 1.5 Nobel Winner Svante Pääbo Discovered the Neandertal in Our Genes by Daniela Mocker (October 4, 2022); 1.6 Piltdown Man Came from The Lost World... Well, No, It Didn't by Darren Naish (October 9, 2015); 2.1 What Makes the Human Footprint Unique? by Krystal D'Costa (October 3, 2018); 2.2 What Made Us Unique by Kevin Laland (September 1, 2018); 2.3 Is "Junk DNA" What Makes Humans Unique? by Zach Zorich (January 30, 2018); 2.4 What Makes Humans Different Than Any Other Species by Gary Stix (September 1, 2014); 3.1 Ancient Stone Tools Force Rethinking of Human Origins by Kate Wong (May 1, 2017); 3.2 The Other Tool Users by Michael Haslam (March 1, 2019); 3.3 Early Butchers Used Small Stone Scalpels by Christopher Intagliata (September 18, 2019); 3.4 Stone Age String Strengthens Case for Neandertal Smarts by Kate Wong (April 9, 2020); 3.5 Is This Going to Be a Stand-Up Fight, Sir, or Another Sloth Hunt? by Riley Black (May 18, 2018); 3.6 Origins of Creativity by Heather Pringle (October 1, 2016); 3.7 Mind Your "Fs" and "Vs": Agriculture May Have Shaped Both Human Jaws and Language by Anna Pycha (March 14, 2019); 3.8 The Cultural Origins of Language by Christine Kenneally (September 1, 2018); 3.9 An Ancient Proto-City Reveals the Origin of Home by Annalee Newitz (March 1, 2021); 4.1 Case for (Very) Early Cooking Heats Up by Kate Wong (September 1, 2013); 4.2 Human Evolution Led to an Extreme Thirst for Water by Asher Y. Rosinger (July 1, 2021); 4.3 Our 14,400-Year-Old Relationship with Bread by Krystal D'Costa (July 24, 2018)

Each author biography was accurate at the time the article was originally published.

INDEX